gift fro
Pine
C

GENTLEMEN OF MERSTHAM
AND GATTON
1519 to 1979

GENTLEMEN OF MERSTHAM AND GATTON

1519 to 1979

A. B. de M. Hunter

The Book Guild Ltd.
Sussex, England

The Book Guild Ltd.,
25 High Street,
Lewes, Sussex.

First published 1993
© A. B. de M. Hunter 1992
Set in Baskerville
Typesetting by R & H Typesetters
Horley, Surrey.

Printed in Great Britain by
Antony Rowe Ltd.
Chippenham, Wiltshire.

A catalogue record for this book is
available from the British Library

ISBN 0 86332 801 6

CONTENTS

LIST OF ILLUSTRATIONS

PRINCIPAL FAMILIES

Period:	Tudor	Stuart	Hanoverian	Victorian	Windsor
	COPLEY	TURGIS/NEWLAND	COLEBROOKE	MONSON	COLMAN
	SOUTHWELL		DOCMINIQUE		
		SOUTHCOTE		JOLLIFFE	
Dates:	1500	1600	1700	1800	1900

8

INTRODUCTION

Given its strategic position at a dip in the Downs, due south
of London, it is surprising to find that, while similar Downs
villages have grown into such towns as Dorking or
Caterham, Merstham remains relatively compact and
undeveloped. Indeed Gatton, a neighbouring hamlet linked
to Merstham for ecclesiastical purposes, would have long
disappeared had it not been for its dubious status as a
Parliamentary borough for most of the period under review.
That they continue to maintain their separate identities,
rather than be absorbed into the spreading conurbation of
Redhill/Reigate, is a relic of the Green Belt policy of the
last fifty years. That they never developed into a town of
comparable size is a reflection of the differing intentions,
and fortunes, of the gentlemen who owned these Downs
domains. The history of these estates is the story of their
owners.

Any history of Surrey landowners cannot easily be
separated from the history of the country as a whole, and
Merstham and Gatton being only 16 miles from the capital,
were owned by men caught up in some of the major events
of their time. These local gentlemen, and their ladies, are
more interesting than famous, diverse yet representative
of the broadly defined 'landed gentry' that determined
England's historical development over the last 500 years.
Whether a Cavalier or a Canadian, nabob or navvy,
Regency rake or Royalty, admiral or antiquary, manufacturer or merchant, Merstham and Gatton have seen them
all. This is the best sketch possible on the available
evidence, to help explain the character of a typical English

village, and, in doing so, illustrate how one microscopic element fits into the broader historical context.

In compiling this, there are many to whom I am much indebted. This book is my 'thank you' to all of them, some for editing the bits with which they are familiar, and some for merely giving me the encouragement to get the task done. Of the former I am especially grateful to Joyce Milsom for making available the scrapbooks of Mrs Gwynne; of the latter I pay tribute to the patience and support of my wife Ruth. This book is otherwise dedicated to the ghosts that flit around the local landmarks!

A. B. de M. Hunter
Merstham 1990

I

ROYAL FAVOURS
1519-1549

By 1519 Henry VIII had reigned for a decade, and Merstham had been owned by Christchurch abbey, Canterbury, for 500 years. The earliest reference to Merstham is in a land charter of 675AD, while Gatton is referred to in a similar document of about 880AD. Even without such references, their Saxon names alone rank them among the oldest villages in Surrey, but we have been left no record of the character, or characters, of these villages until the traumas of the Tudor period created the legal and political requirement to keep documentary evidence. At this stage of Henry VIII's reign, the pride and joy of these neighbouring communities would have been their parish churches. Both hamlets had had a church since at least the Domesday Survey of 1086, and some idea of the relative size of each community can be judged from the thirteenth century enlarged church of St Katharine's at Merstham compared to the largely fifteenth century, but smaller layout, of St Andrew's church at Gatton. Both churches owed their origin, and most of their endowment, to their position beside the 'Old Road'. Along this track as far back as history can trace, pack horses had carried their burdens east/west on the high dry turf of the chalk downlands between woods to the north and marshes to the south. Further east along the route the traveller would find himself increasingly on Canterbury-owned land, whether by abbey or cathedral, and the accommodation at Otford, where the Londoners joined the road, and beyond, was literally palatial. Christchurch, Canterbury, was a Benedictine monastery with its origins going back to the re-establishment of Christianity by St Augustine in 597. For centuries it had provided its several estates with monks dispensing alms and education, ministering to the souls and bodies of its tenants and servants. Though the gradual change from feudal serfdom to yeoman tenancy had weakened the Church's direct involvement with the administration of its lands, its temporal authority was as unquestioned as its spiritual. Originally Merstham manor's rent had been assessed as enough to clothe a few monks, but over time the country had become more prosperous and the prelates' demands on behalf of their monarch more exacting. Apart from the traditional agricultural living from sheep on the Downs and crops in the Bottom (Saxon for a cultivated valley), and a reasonable trade from the pilgrims and other travellers to Canterbury and the coast, the parish boasted a thriving stone works, previously used for Westminster Palace and Windsor Castle and presently for Nonesuch Palace, which could well have been its main source of income.

Two very different families shaped the fortunes of Merstham and Gatton in the half century prior to Henry VIII's reign. Up on the Downs, William Best tenanted Alderstead sub manor, controlling the surrounding woods and pastures and paying rent to Canterbury, but otherwise independent of any feudal lord. It is ironic that one of his family, Thomas Best of nearby Caterham, had sworn to the peace in Surrey in 1434, yet his kinsman, possibly a son, Thomas Best of Lewes, had to be pardoned for being out with Cade in the rebellion and possession of London in 1450. It is quite possible that Merstham men were thus involved in that uprising and plundering. By contrast both Gatton and the Albury sub-manor of Merstham were part of a wider area under the protection of the Dukes of Norfolk through their retainer, John Timperley and his same-named son. Both Johns had made improvements to Reigate and Merstham, but it was at tiny but safer Gatton, in between the two, that the father established in 1450 (after the rising) with royal consent, his parliamentary 'borough', known for a while as 'Timperley's Town'. By coming to terms with Henry VI, John Timperley, otherwise a staunch Yorkist, kept Merstham peaceful during the Wars of the Roses. His reliance on the Duke of Norfolk was noted in the 1452 description of him as 'late of Framlington (Norfolk's castle), alias of Merstham, Esquire'. But with the temporary fall of Norfolk in 1485 the Timperley leases were no longer united by 'livery and maintenance' so that by Henry VIII's time the old Timperley manors were rented by different families more independent of each other. Nevertheless the Duke of Norfolk continued to list Gatton among his dozen or so controlled Parliamentary boroughs.

The only qualified voting inhabitant at Gatton by then was Sir Roger Copley, High Sheriff of Surrey and Sussex, who had received the manor from his late brother Richard's wife in 1518. These Copleys were originally from Doncaster (where a branch of the family stayed) but had become established wool merchants in London since at least 1456 when the first Sir Roger Copley had been granted the freedom of the Mercers' Company. The Mercers', Grocers', Drapers', and to a lesser extent Fishmongers' and Goldsmiths' livery companies ruled London and wisely kept it neutral in the rivalries that surrounded the Crown. In particular, certain wool merchants, the Merchants of the Staple, which included the Copleys, enjoyed an export trading monopoly guaranteed by Royal charter in return for providing the monarchy with funding from time to time. This merchant aristocracy had its houses and agents in Antwerp, Bruges and Calais, operating their own vessels from the Pool of London, and managed the commercial wealth of the country. Not that there was any distinction then between moneyed and landed: Sir Roger Copley had acquired through marriage to Anne, the co-heiress of Lord Hoo, her lands at Roffey, Horsham, and in 1472 the family acquired the rights to the Maze and Ewell manors in Southwark. Then a kinsman from Lewes priory, Edward Copley, was appointed rector of Merstham in 1488, conveniently between the two estates. It was probably through this introduction to the area that Copley acquired first the leasehold and then the freehold of Gatton from the Timperleys. Relying on the 1562 Visitation rather than later pedigrees, the first Sir Roger that took on Gatton was different to and father of Roger that ran the 'borough' in the 1540s.

A rental document of 1522 shows the two main sub-manors of Merstham, Alderstead and Albury, to be tenanted by Richard Best and John Dannett respectively. Richard was the latest of the long-established Best family already mentioned. The Dannetts were of Leicestershire origin. John's father, Gerard Dannett, had been a member of Henry VII's household who had married Sir Edward Belknap's sister. Both John and his brother, Thomas, had married into Surrey families. Thomas married Anne Browne of Betchworth, while John married his ward, Anne Elingbridge (one would like to think a willing bride) and thus acquired her properties of Croham, Chaldon and Albury manors. John followed his father into the King's household and was knighted by Henry VIII for his services at York Place (later called Whitehall) in 1529. One of several other gentlemen knighted at the same time was William Shelley of Michelgrove and Leigh Place, connected to the Mercers' Company and Justice of the Common Pleas, whose marriage to Alice Belknap made him a relative of the Dannetts of Albury. There were several other tenants mentioned in the Merstham rental but with much less substantial acreage. Here, as throughout most of Tudor England, the resentment of the Church as landlord was the one common factor between such diverse tenants as the yeomen Bests and the Dannett courtiers. The families were well established; their wealth and learning more recent. Indeed it was just this increasing attraction of such secular pursuits that led to the reduction in quantity and quality of churchmen, sapping the efficiency rather than morality of the English Church.

The first half of Henry VIII's reign was characterised by both the import of the effect of the Renaissance and the export of England's wealth to support the fluctuating papal policy in Europe. Craftsmanship flourished, so that the typical trappings of a parish church such as St Katharine's was the envy of the Venetian ambassador of the time, while the increasing tax demands of Wolsey's Commissioners for his foreign schemes were the curse of every Englishman.

14

Relief was expected with the Peace of Cambrai and the fall of Wolsey. As a Justice of the Common Pleas it was the recently knighted Sir William Shelley who was sent with the Duke of Norfolk to demand the surrender of York Place from Wolsey in October 1529. Sir Thomas More took the oath of Lord Chancellor days later, symbolically the first secular Chancellor since Edward the Confessor's day. Merstham's gentry were not immediately involved with the new order, Roger Copley letting two other Surrey magnates, Saunders and Guildford, use his Gatton parliamentary seats for the anti-clerical legislation of November that year. Henry VIII's isolation of, and supremacy over, the Church in England was a gradual affair intended initially to force and finally to by-pass the need for a papal annulment of his son-less marriage. Not until 1533, with More retired, Cranmer as Archbishop of Canterbury and Anne Boleyn pregnant, was the long business of the divorce finalised. As Anne Boleyn's great-grandmother was another co-heiress of Lord Hoo, the Shelleys could now expect to be much favoured at Court, despite Cromwell's antipathy for Sir William. Roger Copley must therefore have congratulated himself on his marriage about this time to Elizabeth Shelley, Sir William's daughter. His sister Mary married Thomas Shelley, Elizabeth's brother. Through this alliance with the Shelleys, the Copleys were now thus related to their neighbours, the Dannetts. Family ties were important in cementing the common interests of these new Surrey and Sussex land-owning families of Shelley and Copley, Gage (who was related to the Bests) and Saunders (also related to the Dannetts). Sir John Dannett's only son, Leonard, and Roger Copley's first child, Bridget, were born shortly before the birth of their distant cousin, Princess Elizabeth, in September 1533. Roger Copley's son and heir, Thomas, was born a year or two later.

Meanwhile the Act of Supremacy was put on the statute books in 1534. Presumably locals and travellers through Merstham were wont to refer to the King and his recent bride as heretic or schismatic, as in the rest of the country, for the Treason Act of his session made such oral or written references treasonable. As will been seen, it is significant to the future history of the Copley family that one of those

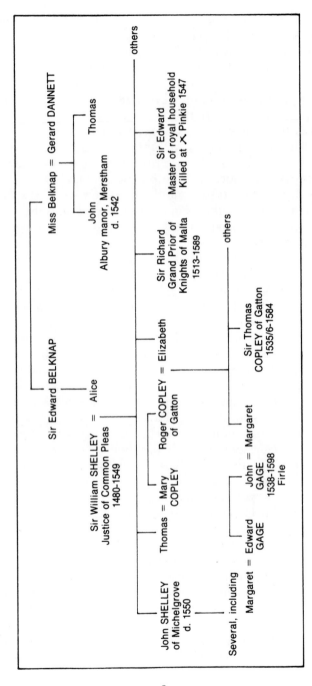

Sir Edward BELKNAP

Miss Belknap = Gerard DANNETT

Sir William SHELLEY = Alice
Justice of Common Pleas
1480-1549

John SHELLEY
of Michelgrove
d. 1550

Thomas = Mary
COPLEY

Roger COPLEY = Elizabeth
of Gatton

John
Albury manor, Merstham
d. 1542

Thomas

Sir Edward
Master of royal household
Killed at ✕ Pinkie 1547

Sir Richard
Grand Prior of
Knights of Malta
1513-1589

others

Sir Thomas
COPLEY of Gatton
1535/6-1584

others

Several, including
Margaret = Edward
GAGE

John = Margaret
GAGE
1538-1598
Firle

16

brought to trial under this Act was a William Copley, a Yorkshire cousin of Roger and a member of Gray's Inn. For him the matter was clearcut: 'If there be no pope, there can be no bishop, and if there be no bishop, there can be no priest, and if there be no priest, there can be no saved souls', and, in his opinion, 'the Queen's Grace should not be called Queen Anne, but Anne the bawd'. Respect for the law was such, however, that opposition was limited to those few who, in matters of principle, rated their consciences higher than the law of the land. And the Law was increasingly a more prosperous occupation for the new gentry than the traditional trades. Sir William Shelley played his part on the bench at the trials of Bishop Fisher, and of the Carthusian monks, but not of Sir Thomas More, in 1535.

One of those who refused to perjure himself at Thomas More's notorious trial was Richard Southwell, thirty-one and one of the recently appointed Royal Commissioners to investigate the Church's property values. He and his younger brothers, Robert and Francis, were well brought up to the task, their late father having been Auditor of the Exchequer, and themselves being brought up as wards of the Howards of Norfolk. Richard was a headstrong young man, having two years previously been pardoned for complicity in a murder, and already with some illegitimate children by his future second wife, Mary Darcy, kinswoman to his first wife, Thomasin Darcy. He was already one of the wealthier of Henry's courtiers with estates in Norfolk (Woodrising), and Suffolk (Barham Hall). As part of Cromwell's team the Southwells took a safely pragmatic approach to politics while the more partisan Howards, Shelleys and Copleys took a lower profile following the disgrace and execution of Anne Boleyn. Sir William had to take part in her trial though.

As always politics mattered less to local folk than economics. Another statute of 1534 had imposed a greater level of tax on the Church than was ever required by Rome. As a monastic fief, Merstham did not feel the burden of this. The monastic orders did not answer to the Bishops so that their continuing autonomy denied the King both their potential revenue and his authority. Such could not

Sir Richard Southwell
1504-1564
Brother of Sir Robert Southwell, Merstham's first
private owner, and future father-in-law of Bridget
Copley of Gatton.

last. The visitations by the Commissioners were followed in 1536 by the dissolution of initially the smaller monastic institutions. Despite the careful manner in which it was carried out (with monastic debts, and monks if not their lay staff, properly seen to), there was no escaping the sudden destruction of centuries old communities and landmarks. Thomas Cromwell's designs on the country's traditional religious institutions created a reaction across the country and prompted the rising in the North called the Pilgrimage of Grace. The Duke of Norfolk, who commanded the King's forces, reported that he could not stand against the rebels and that there 'were right few of the common soldiers in his army that did not think the cause of the Northern men good and godly'. The King was compelled to bargain with the rebels and 'promise them what they would ask'. Not that he did so: the leaders of the Pilgrimage of Grace, and of the Walsingham rising the following year, were arrested and executed throughout 1537. Amongst those executed were the abbots of several of the larger monastic houses, paving the way for their dissolution the following year. As in the case of the pilgrimage centre at Walsingham, the shrine of St Thomas at Canterbury, described by the Venetian ambassador as the finest in the land, was destroyed and all images or written references to him prohibited. St Thomas's martyrdom, of course, had been in the interest of the liberty of the Church in England. For Merstham this meant the removal of the Thomas chapel fittings and, with Cromwell's anti-pilgrimage legislation of 1536, a sudden dearth of lucrative pilgrim traffic. Locals may have benefited from the former, but not the latter. Equally, whether related to the dissolution or not, there was a steady increase in sturdy beggars that gave cause for concern for such roadside villages as Merstham. The villagers' sense of insecurity was somewhat calmed by Sir John Dannett's review of his thirty-eight armed men that year. After all, the King's great matter had been settled with the birth of Prince Edward, and religious orthodoxy within the new English Church maintained with the 'Bishops' book' (a bible translated into English). Of all Surrey only three men (a knight hospitaller, a Franciscan friar and the vicar of Wandsworth) were executed for their scruples over the King's religious supremacy.

With the dissolution of Christchurch, Canterbury, in 1539 Merstham was part of the estates that fell to the Crown, which never intended, nor could afford, to keep all such sequestrated lands. In return for other property, the ex-monastic estates of Charlewood and Merstham were granted in August by the King to Sir Robert Southwell, Richard's younger brother and rival in wealth from dissolved monasteries in Norfolk, Suffolk, Essex, London, Kent, Surrey, and Sussex. He would appear to be a more stable character than his elder brother, being tutor to young Gregory Cromwell, member of the 1536 Parliament, and married to Margaret, heiress of Sir Thomas Neville. He may well have received his knighthood through the patronage of Sir Anthony Browne. It would be reasonable to assume that the Bests and Dannetts were relieved to have an absentee landlord of such means and character. Certainly the Southwells did not suffer from the fall of their patron, Cromwell, in 1540, Sir Robert became Master of the Rolls and Chancellor of the powerful Court of Augmentations that year.

Nevertheless few could feel secure near such a fearful monarch. The 3rd Duke of Norfolk felt more secure with a second of his nieces married to the King. His brother, William Howard became a neighbour of the Copleys with the acquisition of Reigate's dissolved Priory at this time. But, like Anne Boleyn before her, Catherine Howard soon fell out of favour and her family was disgraced. This did not damage the careers of their erstwhile playmates, the Southwells. In 1542 Richard Southwell was finally knighted and his brother Francis appointed to their father's former post, Auditor of the Exchequer. Sir Robert later gained the Howard's Kentish property of Badlesmere. As they had shared childhoods and their grandsons were to enjoy a future relationship, it is ironic that it was Sir Richard Southwell who was the accuser of the vulnerable Howards alleging he knew things touching on the fidelity of Henry Howard, Earl of Surrey. Henry, with every bit as headstrong a reputation as Richard, did not improve his position by asking in vain to fight Richard 'in his shirt'. In January 1547 Henry and his father, the Duke of Norfolk, were indicted for high treason, the son for merely displaying the Royal Arms, the father for failing to reveal the offence. The death of the King intervened in time to save the father from the capital fate of his son, though he did stay imprisoned throughout Edward's reign. Henry Howard's orphaned children joined their aunt, Mary Fitzroy, in Reigate Castle.

The way in which Henry VIII devoted the remaining years of his reign to suppressing political and religious extremes of whatever hue, was of less concern to Merstham tenants after the confusion of the traumatic earlier years. In any event the rapid inflation and series of coinage debasements from 1544 made more material matters the topic of conversation in the ale houses. Gatton was relatively neglected because Roger Copley, recently granted his father's membership of the Mercers' Company, divided his time between his Roffey and Southwark estates, and his wife's small 200-acre estate at Leigh Place. In March 1544, though, the Copleys sold part of their Southwark interests (the modern Hays Wharf complex by London Bridge) for £200. The growth of large unit sheep farming at the expense of arable smallholdings that so much changed other parts of England, hardly affected Merstham. This is partly because the gradient of the downlands naturally favoured pasture as opposed to tillage, partly because Timperley had already enclosed parkland at Albury and Gatton, and partly because revenues from Merstham stone were inflation-proof. The demand for the limited amount of stone in the area for the new gentry's manor houses was affordable out of their income from the increased litigation and trade in land. It was one such newly wealthy lawyer, Sir Thomas Saunders of Charlewood, who acquired the advowson of Merstham in 1544 from the Archbishop of Canterbury. The document, signed by Thomas Cranmer, exists still at the British Museum.

When Sir John Dannett died, it is likely his wife had the 12-year-old Leonard Dannett complete his education with his Copley cousins. Not that Sir Roger long survived his neighbour or his monarch. He died in 1548 and was buried in St Olave's church (which used to be in Tooley Street next to Old London Bridge). His father-in-law died only months later. Roger Copley had been a man of learning, well exposed to the Renaissance through both his own continental commercial activities, and his wife's family. Two of his brothers-in-law were distinguished knights of St John (Sir Richard Shelley was the first Englishman to visit Constantinople since its capture by the Turks) while another was master of Henry VIII's household who also did not long survive his monarch, being killed at the Battle of Pinkie in 1547. The Copley children were much influenced by their mother, Elizabeth, a redoubtable woman who was allowed to 'vote' her members of Parliament for Gatton hundreds of years before women were legally entitled to! Nor did her children (see family tree, p.30) lack talent. Bridget, in particular, had a reputation for intelligence and a cousin of hers, Princess Elizabeth, was to refer to her as 'my very learned lady and Latin tutor'. Typically the next stage of the young gentlemen's education was the Inns of Court, at a time when the country, and London in particular, was to be embroiled in further religious and political turmoil.

2

FAMILY TIES
1550-1570

Into the vacuum following Henry VIII's death had passed
the ruinous self-interest of powerful bodies, which Henry,
for all his faults, had kept in check. Agrarian and religious
grievances came to the fore with risings in Cornwall and
Norfolk. For these few years of Edward's reign continental
reformers flocked to England, though rarely settling beyond
Kent, London and East Anglia. John Foxe returned from
Geneva and was employed as tutor to the young Howards
at Reigate Castle. The first stage of the doctrinal
Reformation was the Prayer Book of 1549 enforced by an
Act of uniformity. Sir Richard Southwell spent a year or so
in Fleet prison probably not so much a reflection on his
religious tastes as a political convenience, given his
opposition to the King's uncle and Protector. Sir Robert
Southwell having learnt from his brother's imprisonment
resigned from public office in 1550 and retired to his Kent
property. With the revised Prayer Book of 1552, the 42
Articles of the following year and the replacement of most of
the bishops, the Reformation had come to England with a
rapidity that surprised all but the London-based populace.
Young Thomas Copley was one of those caught up in the
new movement, convincing his mother to let Reverend
Thomas Marten, a protégé of the ardent reformer, Bishop
Poynet, have the Gatton living in 1552. The family-run
parish was apparently ill-endowed. The 1552 return to the

Commissioners responsible for assessing potential proceeds from the sale of Church ornaments listed "rotten" vestments, "ragged" altar cloths, a chalice borrowed from Chipstead and a bell not loud enough *"to be heard a flight schotte agaynst the wynde"* but perhaps Lady Copley had set it up so for their visit. At Merstham the sale of its remaining Church valuables included the stone altar which Richard Best of Alderstead bought for 13s 4d.

With the demise of King Edward early in 1553, however, the Reformation seemed doomed to be a minority movement, committed English Protestants being fewer than in France, the southern Netherlands or Bavaria. Certainly there was no doubt about the enthusiasm at Mary's accession. Her first Parliament that March repealed the Edwardian legislation, returning the country to the 1547 position. Lady Copley had voted Leonard Dannett (now a member of Middle Temple) and Sir Richard's eldest son, Richard Southwell, as members for Gatton. Richard Southwell, though illegitimate, had been granted his father's Horsham St Faith estate in Norfolk under a settlement of his father in 1545 (most of his vast estates later passed to his nearest legitimate relative, nephew Thomas). Even so, Richard was not obviously the best match for well-connected and regarded Bridget Copley, so that their marriage at this time may well have been based more on mutual regard than as a convenient alliance.

Some continuity in policy, and security of land tenure, was Parliament's main concern in petitioning for Mary's early marriage though there was bound to be opposition to whoever she chose. Her proposed marriage to Philip of Spain, as planned by Henry VIII in 1525, under terms that gave Philip no rights over England, was sound politics. Until the revolt of the Spanish Netherlands in the following reign, Spain was England's natural ally against her traditional enemy, France. Nevertheless the foreign match was not popular. In January 1554, the Duke of Suffolk, whose first rebellion had been pardoned, proclaimed Lady Jane Grey again in Leicestershire while Sir Thomas Wyatt raised Kent. The Dannetts and the Southwells were, for family reasons, in opposite camps. If Merstham men were involved, they were more likely to follow the local tenant than absent landlord. Reigate was united under James Skinner and William Howard who immediately arrested a friend of Copley's, Sir Thomas Cawarden, Master of the Revels and custodian of the ex queen Anne of Cleves at Bletchingley for suspected complicity in the rising. They confiscated enough arms to equip 110 horse and over 300 foot. Being related through the Wootons to the Duke of Suffolk, Leonard Dannett and his uncle joined his brief and futile rising. Indicted for their part in February, both Dannetts spent some months in the Tower of London before receiving a Royal pardon, in May for Leonard, and October for his uncle Thomas. Meanwhile Sir Robert Southwell and his father-in-law, Lord Abergavenny, had achieved some initial success in Kent, but their retainers soon lost heart when faced with Wyatt's militia which he had been training since 1549. The old Duke of Norfolk, released from the Tower a couple of years earlier, was sent out with the London-trained band to quell his last revolt but also found his force more ready to join than oppose Wyatt's growing numbers. Only when the City of London denied him access, did Wyatt's progress lose momentum. His forces were soon dispersed and defeated. William Howard was made Lord Howard of Effingham for his part. The prospect of more uprisings such as by Cade had severely shocked the Government and it reacted by persecuting those Protestants whom it considered dangerous to the public peace. It was these persecutions (much publicised by Foxe writing from Strasbourg, Frankfurt and Basle since his eviction from Reigate by the Duke of Norfolk), for which Mary's reign was later to be best known. Yet for all the fires in London, and Lewes, there were none in between. Marten kept his Gatton living, while it would appear to be natural causes that put John Wystow into the Merstham living in 1557. Despite Foxe's sojourn in Reigate, there is little trace of Protestant opinion in Surrey during Mary's reign.

Thomas Copley, meanwhile, had come of age and elected himself for both Parliamentary sessions of 1554. He was quick enough to take advantage of Wyatt's rising and gained Rochester House from Bishop Poynet who had sided with the rebels. Admitted young by special licence to Inner Temple, he consorted with Thomas Norton, a relative of

Cranmer's and later infamous as Elizabeth's zealous rackmaster. Indeed the pair gained such a reputation for "wilful demeanor and disobedience" that they were both expelled from Inner Temple in 1556 and spent some time cooling off in Fleet prison. Backed by his late father's fortune, Thomas was soon back enjoying "costly building, chargeable music, horses and such like vanities as my age delighted in". The following year saw England's disastrous involvement in the Franco-Spanish conflict which stretched the limited resources of Mary's government. Although Calais had become less important to the English cloth merchants than Antwerp, it was traditionally the main base of the Merchants of the Staple. Typical of that powerful clique, Copley felt betrayed by the Crown when Calais was virtually abandoned to the French. This national disgrace, and the Queen's clear lack of fertility, focused ambitious young minds on the heir apparent, Princess Elizabeth. Thomas Copley elected his friend Thomas Norton as his fellow member for Gatton in Mary's fourth Parliament. At the formal introduction to this 1558 session he expressed dutiful affection in such a disloyal manner as to lead to another brief term in prison. No sooner was he out than he made another error of judgement: He turned down the hand of the daughter of his neighbour, Lord Howard of Effingham, thus making a lifelong enemy of Princess Elizabeth's champion, soon to be the most powerful man in the land. In July 1558, Thomas chose instead to marry Catherine, eldest daughter of the late Sir John Luttrell of Dunster Castle in Somerset, and a much sought-after beauty. At any rate she must be the reason why, within the space of a few months, this idle young rebel had matured into a responsible member of the establishment. For he was then appointed to join the royal commissioners negotiating for peace on the continent. In November Queen Mary died, having named Elizabeth her successor. Young Copley was sent back to England with letters of congratulation to the new Queen, and was immediately appointed to the Surrey Commission of the Peace.

In May 1559 another Copley was married, Margaret, one of Thomas' three sisters, married John, eldest son and heir of Sir Edward Gage, Sheriff of Surrey and Sussex. Her mother, Lady Elizabeth Copley, was now the dowager of the family and began to extend the estates on behalf of her future heirs. Accordingly she bought him the "farm and tenements" of Chipstead (which she referred to as being in Merstham in her will that December), from Leonard Dannett, who may well have been financially embarrassed by his lack of court office. In due course Dannett was given some role in local administration, but the new Queen did not have to rely on her previous supporters. There were sufficient members of the establishment who had dutifully served Henry, Edward and Mary without qualm to provide a backbone to the new regime, men such as Petre, Cecil, Mason and Rich who were "sprung from the willow rather than the oak".

At Elizabeth's accession England was a Catholic country, allied to Spain whose Netherlands province was still its main trading outlet, and fearful of France united with Scotland in July 1559 under the same Queen, Mary Stuart, the half-French cousin of Elizabeth and nearest claimant to the English throne. Indeed, if Elizabeth was regarded as illegitimate, it was possible to argue that Mary Stuart had a better claim than Elizabeth. As in the case of Mary Tudor before her, Elizabeth's right to the throne rested on the religious legality of her mother's marriage. The re-establishment of Protestant doctrine was thus her first priority. Thomas Copley was a member of her first Parliament that voted her "Supreme Governor" of the English Church, Saunders saying later that many found it more tolerable than "Supreme Head". With similar compromises in the Queen's Injunctions of that year, the gentry had little difficulty in falling in with the new order, though all the bishops ended up in the Tower, to be replaced largely by former exiles.

Initially there was little change with Elizabeth's accession in the parishes of Merstham and Gatton. On Christmas Day 1559 Elizabeth Copley died, leaving her estates to Thomas. She was buried next to her husband at St Olave's, Southwark. Within months Sir Robert Southwell was also dead. His eldest son, Thomas Southwell, already had Hoxon Hall in Suffolk, so Sir Robert willed in August 1559 *that where my wife Dame Margarett standeth and is seased as joynt purchaser with me for terme of her life of and in the manor of Merstham al's Mestham with appurt's in Surrey, . . the manor to after her death to my two sonnes Frauncis and Robert for their lives, according to an estate thereof executed in my lif to John Nevill and others by deade of feoffment enrolled in the chauncery".*[1] One begins to understand the living available to lawyers of the period. For the time being Nicholas Best and Leonard Dannett paid their rent to Sir Robert's widow. The last of the Copley's sisters, Katherine, was married to Sir Robert Lane from Northamptonshire at about this time. The parishes were visited by the commissioners enforcing the Act of Uniformity and subsequent Thirty-Nine Articles: John Wystow stayed on as the Merstham rector but one Robert Copley, presumably related, was deprived of his living at Walton-on-the-Hill, as was Henry Norman, parson of Reigate, in 1562. Gatton's Thomas Marten was dead by then. Weekly attendance of the new service was enforced, absentees fined and refusers entered on the sheriff's "Recusant rolls". Pretence was not an option; that year the Pope forbade Catholics to attend Anglican Matins. The religious polarisation (so strange and tragic when viewed in the light of current ecumenical trends) that was to overshadow Merstham for the next century, was then seen to be inevitable. For, as William Cecil believed, "the state could never be in safety where there was toleration of two religions. For there is no emnity so great as that for religion, and they that differ in the service of God can never agree in the service of their country". According to a Spanish ambassador Thomas Copley opted for the Catholic way of religion in 1563. Robert Parsons, a Jesuit, suggested it was occasioned by Bishop Jewell's inability to refute, at Robert Dudley's dinner table, Copley's criticism of the bishop's newly published *Apologia*. For a while the matter was viewed as a permissible academic eccentricity in an otherwise valuable member of the Queen's government in Surrey.

Copley, recently granted membership of the Mercers' Company, now voted himself and his brother-in-law, Robert Lane, to the 1563 Parliament. Leonard Dannett had to find another seat (Marlborough) this time. All three thus took part in what turned out to be the greatest output of economic legislation that had ever been passed at a single session. For the next few years Copley busied himself with his growing family, his Justice of the Peace duties and his business interests. He extended his estates with the purchase of neighbouring Reigate and Colley manors in 1566. When Margaret Southwell, Robert's wife, died in 1569, the two sons that were now entitled to Merstham in their father's will, alienated the reversion to Thomas Copley, being related through their cousin Richard's marriage to Bridget Copley. Thomas entered into occupation after a certain amount of difficulty with his new tenants, the Bests. Nicholas Best had died in 1566, leaving his Nutfield and Alderstead tenancies to his three sons, Christopher, William and Henry. It was Christopher Best's eldest daughter, Alice, and her husband William Richbell, who tried to imply greater tenancy rights than Thomas Copley was prepared to give. With the Queen as godmother to his eldest son and heir, Henry, and one of his uncles, Sir Richard Shelley, as grand prior of the Knights of St John, in Venice, Copley could claim some powerful connections. He was even distantly related to William Cecil, the Queen's most able minister. Thus, when Mary Stuart took refuge in 1568 in England from her rebellious subjects, Copley was not one of those attracted to her as the focal point of dissent (the way Elizabeth had been under Mary Tudor, and Mary Tudor under Edward), nor was he connected with the rising of the Northern earls the following year.

This rising was a provincial and conservative reaction to the rapid social changes of the period and not primarily, as in 1536, on religious grounds. It had the effect however of planting in the public mind the association of Catholicism with political treason which was to prove irradicable for generations. The previous year's sudden determination of Thomas Copley to do more than merely hold academic sympathies for Catholics has been charitably described by a recent political biographer as 'spectacularly ill-timed'. For he had already been given a warning (with yet another short term in prison) in 1568 for giving financial aid to English Catholics abroad in Louvain. Yet the following year his Southwark manager, Donald Sharples, noted in the accounts:[2] *Paid to Mr Cooke, keeper of the goal at Southwark,*

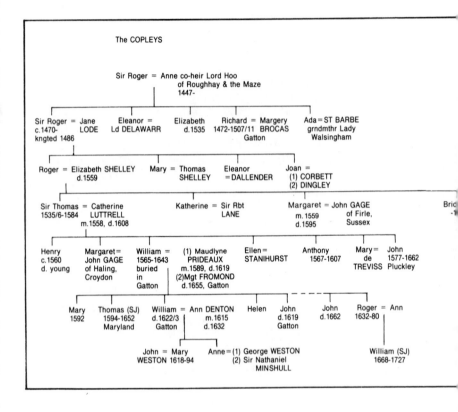

The COPLEYS

Sir Roger = Anne co-heir Lord Hoo
of Roughhay & the Maze
1447-

Sir Roger = Jane   Eleanor =   Elizabeth   Richard = Margery   Ada = ST BARBE
c.1470-   LODE   Ld DELAWARR   d.1535   1472-1507/11 BROCAS   grndmthr Lady
kngted 1486   Gatton   Walsingham

Roger = Elizabeth SHELLEY   Mary = Thomas   Eleanor   Joan =
        d.1559   SHELLEY   = DALLENDER (1) CORBETT
                                                            (2) DINGLEY

Sir Thomas = Catherine   Katherine = Sir Rbt   Margaret = John GAGE   Bric
1535/6-1584 LUTTRELL   LANE   m. 1559   of Firle,   -1
             m.1558, d.1608   d.1595   Sussex

Henry   Margaret =   William =   (1) Maudlyne   Ellen =   Anthony   Mary =   John
c.1560   John GAGE   1565-1643   PRIDEAUX   STANIHURST   1567-1607   de   1577-1662
d. young of Haling,   buried   m.1589, d.1619   TREVISS Pluckley
         Croydon   in   (2)Mgt FROMOND
                      Gatton   d.1655, Gatton

    Mary   Thomas (SJ)   William = Ann DENTON   Helen   John   John   Roger = Ann
    1592   1594-1652   d.1622/3   m.1615   d.1619   d.1662 1632-80
             Maryland   Gatton   d.1632   Gatton

              John = Mary   Anne = (1) George WESTON   William (SJ)
              WESTON 1618-94   (2) Sir Nathaniel   1668-1727
                                       MINSHULL

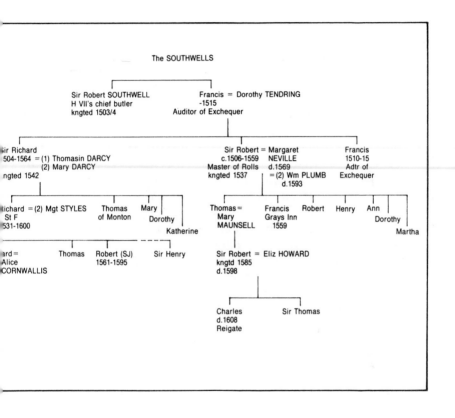

The SOUTHWELLS

Sir Robert SOUTHWELL
H VII's chief butler
kngted 1503/4

Francis = Dorothy TENDRING
-1515
Auditor of Exchequer

Sir Richard
1504-1564 = (1) Thomasin DARCY
          (2) Mary DARCY
kngted 1542

Sir Robert = Margaret
c.1506-1559 NEVILLE
Master of Rolls d.1569
kngted 1537 = (2) Wm PLUMB
                 d.1593

Francis
1510-15
Adtr of
Exchequer

Richard = (2) Mgt STYLES
St F
1531-1600

Thomas
of Monton

Mary
Dorothy
Katherine

Thomas =
Mary
MAUNSELL

Francis
Grays Inn
1559

Robert   Henry   Ann
                   Dorothy
                         Martha

ard =
Alice
CORNWALLIS

Thomas

Robert (SJ)
1561-1595

Sir Henry

Sir Robert = Eliz HOWARD
kngtd 1585
d.1598

Charles
d.1608
Reigate

Sir Thomas

3¹

called the Whyte Lyon, for the chges of 3 prisoners, Ingram, Marshall & Laurance — £3 8s. They were almost certainly impecunious recusants of the lower orders who, removed from their source of earnings would, without such gifts, *'perishe from defayet of Systenauncis'*. To ensure Mr Cooke's co-operation the next entry in the accounts was: *Paid Mr Waye, keeper of the Marshalsea, for 2 prisoners, Richard Cooke and Robert Cooke — 48s 8d!* Despite the recent trading difficulties, with the Spanish Netherlands in revolt, Copley did not lack means. Another £4 10s was duly logged in the accounts as payment for the family's recusant fines of 5s each. As a Justice of the Peace, Copley was bound to take the oath of supremacy, the same supremacy that he had helped enact ten years previously. His letter to his friend, Sir Henry Weston, Sheriff of Surrey, of November that year still exists.[3] In it he states the reasons why he cannot yet be persuaded with safe conscience to comply with the statute and asks to be relieved from the obligation. A man of his position is never without enemies, and Copley was monthly making himself more vulnerable. Interestingly, later in the accounts was a forty shilling expense paid for *'a gonne called a fyer locke pece for Mr Copley'*.

In the spring of 1570 the new Pope decided to excommunicate Queen Elizabeth. This ill-judged papal bull made every English Catholic liable to become a traitor either to his Queen or to his Pope, a dilemma few of them, especially Copley, wanted. Copley's reaction was to quit the country, without the necessary licence, leaving his family and estates safe, as he thought, for the time being. The government then passed the law Mary's government never enacted, enabling the confiscation of the property of exiles. Copley's old enemy, Howard of Effingham, moved quickly to direct the confiscation including "so far a library of books that (Howard) pleasured therewith the universities of England". Further spoilation was averted when Richard Southwell made his home in his brother-in-law's Gatton estate, with, initially, Cecil's approval. The situation was not to be as short term as Copley had hoped. It is from this time that Catholic families began to be excluded from public office, subjected to increasingly severe penalties and, not surprisingly, confine marriages to their own group. A number of Surrey estates that might otherwise be prestigious today began to lose their identity from this point — a benefit, perhaps, to future generations of land-hungry entrepreneurs that made the county the jewel of the home counties.

3

RECUSANTS
1571-1604

It is remarkable that Thomas Copley, who had every
advantage and opportunity in Elizabethan England, should
have so singularly failed to capitalise on them. Intellectually
he was gifted; socially he was well connected with a wide
range of landed might; politically he had identified early in
his career with the future Queen and her prime minister,
both of whom he could claim kinship to; while financially
he had enough City and continental contacts to benefit
from the new opportunities in the changing pattern of trade
of the period. Yet, for fear of compromising his religious
beliefs, he left the country without licence and turned his
back on all this. It is only comprehensible in terms of an
age when the security of one's soul mattered more than
one's body. Certainly the Parliament of this time was under
pressure from the new Puritan element, which, with its own
foreign-based views of the supremacy of Church over State,
posed as much a threat to the government as did the
Papists. Uniform compliance was viewed as vital for the
peace of the realm, and those who obeyed such laws would
'certainly and quietly have and enjoy the fruits of our
former accustomed favour, lenity and grace in all causes
requisite, without any molestation to them by any person by
way of examination or inquisition of their secret opinions in
their consciences, for matters of faith'.
   Armed with this Declaration, Copley sought to be

allowed to return to England without threat of prosecution. On 27th December 1572, he wrote to both Cecil and the Queen:[4] 'My case requires present remedy, and admits no longer delay. I have had not one penny's relief out of England since May twelvemonth. I owe about £400 in this town [Antwerp].' He refers to the proposed confiscation of his Southwark properties, his lean straights, the illegality of the license to travel laws, 'the very laws of England, by an especial proviso in that old servile statute, gave me liberty to pass and repass the seas at pleasure, being free of the Staple, though I have chosen to live after my better calling. Yet I would have not attempted to come without license, considering the general restraint of that old act, if the malicious practices of my enemies had not overtaken me, denying me leisure to follow such a suit, unless I would have tarried with manifest hazard, as at my departure I signified by letter, both to you and the Council, being sorry to be forced to any act that might be drawn to be offensive to you'. Later he was to argue that a royal waiver would not set a precedent as his case was singular: He being of the Staple, his depature was not unlawful. His move was not intended but forced on him. 'It was for want of time, not will, that I stayed not for licence'.

In the absence of any favourable response Copley offered his services to the Duke of Alva, the Spanish governor of the Netherlands, whose attempt to crush the revised rebellion was already supported by English volunteers. This was possible because distrust of French ambitions and the value of Flemish trade remained more important to Cecil, now Lord Burghley, than religious differences. In 1573 Spain and England promised not to help each other's exiles. Presumably Copley did not fall into this definition of exile, for the following year it was announced in England that King Philip II of Spain had created him Baron Copley of Gatton & Roffey and Master of the Maze [Southwark]! As in the case of his uncle, Sir Richard Shelley, entitled Grand Prior of the Knights of St John, he took care not to use the title to Englishmen out of deference to his Queen.

Merstham tenants were well used to having a non-resident owner (their new rector, Stephen Bateman, who was Archibishop Parker's chaplain, was not much more resident), but it was by no means certain that Copley would be away long. Lord Burghley had allowed the Southwells to occupy the estate to keep a check on the ambitions of the elderly Lord Howard of Effingham, whose grandnephew, the fourth Duke of Norfolk, was suspected and finally executed for treason. But equally, Burghley let the Howards of Effingham nominate under Privy Council instruction a 'good choice of knights and burgesses' for the Gatton Parliamentary seats. When Lord Howard died in 1573, the Southwells' lease arrangement with Copley became less secure, its legality being no longer so necessary in Burghley's delicate balancing act. On a personal level, however, it is clear from the letters that passed between them that Burghley remained well disposed towards Copley, as long as his interests did not conflict with those of state. On 28th December 1574 Burghley wrote to Copley, regretting that for religious scruples he had left his native land, and recommending him to consider the foundations of such a change. His letter ends, however, with a request that Copley give information respecting the authors of the libels of late published against him and the Lord Keeper. Copley's response of 25th February 1575 is interesting:

'I delayed answering yours, being employed in matters of weight for the King, and also I thought my Lord Ambassador was returning, and I could send by him, but he delays; so my service being well completed, I must thank you for yours. I hope my past life will show you my present good meaning, and that you will not have me spoiled of my living for seeking the quiet of my conscience. In Germany the princes use their subjects of whatever religion.

I never begged but one thing of you, and that I obtained, viz. the custody of an idiot, whose living the late Sir T. Saunders was buying for little or nothing to defraud the heir, and then you refused the cup of silver which I offered to show my thankfulness. Also you favoured me in my broils with the late Lord Chamberlain when I was in trouble for religion by my Lord of Canterbury's procurement, at the entreaty of his bedfellow. You also got my sister Gage and her husband licence to pass the seas and live here, all which show your kindness to our cause.

No man can serve two masters and I will not, like some of my countrymen, be false to the good King whom I serve. I wish with you some means were adopted to appease these miserable controversies that rend the Church, and I think such might be devised. The French Huguenots and the rebels of these Low Countries set an example by offering to relent their obstinacy . . You advise me not to favour the Queen's enemies here; this I will avoid more warily than ever. Thanks for your hope of procuring me relief. You ask the author of the book set forth against you and the Lord Keeper in 1572, but I am so unhappy as to be unable to tell you. I think the author knew my alliance to your house and the house of Suffolk but kept it from me as being unlikely to allow it, and I was one of the last that saw it. I believe it was made at home, and not this side of the sea.'

Understandably Burghley was not encouraged by this response and he advised the Earl of Pembroke (who was visiting the peace negotiations at Breda at a time when the rebels were offering the sovereignty of Holland and Zeeland to Queen Elizabeth) to refuse conference or friendship with Mr Copley until he had Her Majesty's favour. Copley treated Pembroke lavishly but was made aware he had detractors. So he wrote in October 1575 to Burghley 'to stop your ears against untrue surmises of me, or keep one open for my justification, and consider the character and motives of persons that slander me. You will always find me true, and I mean by honestly serving the good king who sustains me to win honour to my nation, and yet be a true subject to my own Prince. Pray regard my poor living there, that my houses, rents &c. grow not to decay, to the disherison of my innocent heir, and take order in the Exchequer thereof'. In November he was more specific explaining that he employed English sailors on behalf of

Philip II against his rebels in the best interests of Her Majesty's loyal subjects. 'It is said I fish in troubled waters, but all the waters in Christendom are troubled with faction. I had much rather fish in the calm streams and sweet waters of my own goods in my dear country, when you take compassion on me; but I will withdraw to some state further off, where I may have no likelihood of service offensive to you'. He was still in Antwerp in February 1576; 'Thanks for your goodness. My brother [in law] Gage and my sister are returning to England. I answer your letter sent by them, wishing my return to my country, which you think may be without danger, my fidelity not being doubted, but only my course disliked. Had my case been like my brother's, my return might have shown the *amor patria*, but since I left, a law is passed which on my return, would bind me to yield myself to a bishop, and renounce my faith, than which I would rather beg my bread. Even then I must wait a year before I could enter on my living, and meanwhile could not sustain myself and family'. A month later he reiterated his resolve, as 'it is bootless to strive with a conscience settled in faith, for we daily see men on both sides sustain pains and death with courage. Pray let me have some certainty of my estate.' This Burghley did, for four months later Copley writes with profuse thanks and relief to Burghley. Now he is 'quite content to forbear my rents, to enjoy quiet of conscience and security of person. I do not despair of the Queen's favour to myself or my eldest son, Her Majesty's godson, for some portion of my living. I look upon my being forced to live by foreign service as a punishment for youthful errors.'

The English policy of ensuring that no major nation controlled the Low Countries had been the major reason for providing limited support to Spanish control whenever it seemed unduly threatened. But the increasing success of the Spanish forces in the Netherlands and the growth of the Spanish-allied Guise faction in France meant that the weight of English diplomacy should favour Spain less. Copley was careful to watch out for English interests, even though on the Spanish payroll, and was quick to report how, when in September 1576 he was offered a commission by the Spanish governor to 'levy and take charge of a company of Englishmen on this side of the sea', he remembered his last dealing in a like commission and his promise to the Queen not to meddle more in such service. His discretion was timely. Within months the successful Spanish troops had mutinied and sacked Antwerp, allowing the Prince of Orange to consolidate his position with the Pacification of Ghent, and incidentally ending for good the town's position as England's main trade route. Copley removed his family to the comparative safety of Paris, where the ascendancy of the Guise faction allowed him still to serve Philip of Spain without any conflict of interest with his English ties. These ties were weakened, however, when Henry his eldest son and the Queen's godson, died of pleurisy in Paris. He had other sons (William and Anthony left in England to complete their education, and John who was but newly born), but it is clear that Henry had been the focus of all his father's hopes and aspirations. Copley continued to write to Burghley (who in contrast groomed Robert, his second son, to succeed him in office rather than Thomas, his worthless eldest), but even if he still had the Queen's personal interest, events in England were making his return virtually impossible.

By then the first fifty English Catholic missionaries had slipped back into England with a Counter Reformation zeal that had an effect out of all proportion to their numbers. The fascination for these bright young idealists has been compared to that for the Communist Party of the 1930s. Coinciding as it did with the rise of militant Puritanism, the government could no longer afford the tolerance expressed in the 1570 Declaration. The first seminary priest was executed 'as a terror to the papists' the same year that Archbishop Grindal was suspended for his Puritan sympathies. In May 1576 Richard Southwell was imprisoned in the Marshalsea prison on suspicion of having spoken against the Queen (his wife's childhood friend), and released a few weeks later for lack of evidence. Subsequently his third son, Robert Southwell, who must have been staying with his uncle, Thomas Copley, while completing his studies in Paris, walked to Rome to join the new English Jesuit college there. John Gage's uncle, Robert, was 'the Queen Majesty's prisoner in his own house' for not attending Church, and if

The Copley family in 1580

Sir Thomas and Lady Copley are depicted with their
sons and daughters, alive and dead. The centre shows
the flesh and the devil trying to hold the soul back in
its progress to heaven, but death cuts their cords with
his scythe and the soul ascends through the 13 circles
of the Ptolemaic system. Heaven is arranged in the
Dionysian manner (as in Dante's Divine Comedy).

this was not enough to dissuade Copley from his efforts to return, a special commission into the legal methods of dealing with the recusants, headed by an elderly judge, John Southcote, increased the financial penalties to exorbitant levels.

Perhaps in anticipation of being able to secure the freehold it was this same John Southcote (or Southcott as the family then spelt it) that bought Leonard Dannett's Albury and Chaldon leases in 1579. The Southcotes were a Devon family, John having only recently settled in Witham, Essex, to please his wife, Elizabeth, daughter of a London alderman. He already had other Surrey holdings, including Leigham Place in Streatham, so that the Merstham tenancies may well have been bought for his son and heir, also called John. The son John's marriage to Magdalen, youngest daughter of the late Sir Edward Waldegrave of Hever Castle, is remembered still in their carved initials and arms subsequently incorporated into the East wall of St Katherine's. Leonard's mother, Lady Anne Dannett, had died two years previously. As the last of the Elingbridges and widow of a member of the Tudor Royal household, her funeral was a solemn occasion: *'Mr Morris ye king of Heraulds was here & Mr Blake ye preacher, the bishop of Canterburyes Chaplain.'*[5] Leonard, then about fifty years old and without children, probably moved out of Merstham to join his relatives for the remaining twelve years of his life. The Queen, equally childless, was not much younger, but at an age when previous Tudor monarchs had only a year or two to live. Despite attempts to find the aged queen a husband, there remained no alternative but that her successor would be Mary, the captive and deposed Queen of the Scots.

Thomas Copley still hoped for reconciliation with the existing government, though, and in August 1580, advised Burghley that, as evidence of his loyalty, he was sending his wife home. They parted at Rouen that October, Catherine travelling with the Gages back to England. Her visit did not last long and she stayed mainly with the Whites in Watling Street, London. With the increasing activity of the Catholic seminarist priests, spurred by the recent arrival of Jesuits Campion and Parsons, and the government's fear of a Catholic League similar to that in factious France, England was seething with nervous distrust. No sooner had John Gage reopened Firle Place than he and his brother-in-law, William Shelley, were committed to the Fleet prison for 'obstinancy in Popery'. At the same time the younger generation, Edward Gage and Richard Shelley, were sent to the Marshalsea, a mild prison that by now was quite a resort for Catholic society. The Act of Persuasions passed in 1581 embodies such intolerant penalties that it was only haphazardly applied. The following year Anthony Copley, still a student, stole away from Furnival's Inn to join his parents in Rouen. Even Sir Richard Shelley, who in 1583 had been granted leave to return to England with liberty to practice his religion (for informing on his colleagues which Copley had so determinedly avoided), preferred to stay and die in Venice, once he had heard of the Council's examination of his nephew Richard.

He was predeceased however, by his niece and nephew, Bridget Southwell and her brother Thomas Copley: Thomas died in Flanders on 24th September 1584. Richard Southwell acted as executor of his brother-in-law's will and William Copley, who was then only nineteen, was allowed to inherit his father's estates. Burghley seized the opportunity of William being a minor, though, to direct the sheriff to nominate Burghley's nephew, Francis Bacon, for Gatton's parliamentary seat. In the event Bacon chose to sit for Weymouth instead. Apart from the widowed Catherine the only member of the family who returned to England at this stage was Robert Southwell, by now an ordained Jesuit. He entered the country under the alias of 'Cotton', as it was now an offence punishable by death for an ordained Englishman to re-enter the country.

Merstham's villagers were still without a priest of the established Church, Stephen Bateman preferring his alternate post as Lord Hunsdon's domestic chaplain at Leeds Castle in Kent. Meanwhile priests of the rival firm were busy. In 1584 Justice Southcote's son, John, was reported as having attended mass, whereupon the father resigned his office. His descendants held[10] that his resignation was to avoid having to condemn a priest, and 'bring upon himself and family the guilt of innocent blood. After which he retired to his house at Merstham in Surrey where for three years he led a penitential life and then happily ended his days'. The accuracy of this must be in doubt. For he died in April 1585 and was buried at Whitham where a monument of him in his judge's robes was erected. He was remembered as a 'good natured man, governed by his wife', which had cost him promotion to Lord Chief Justice, as the Queen was reputed to have said that 'she should govern too like a woman, if she suffered a woman to Chief Justice of England'. By then Stephen Bateman had also died, allowing a new, resident, rector, Richard Wood, to be appointed to Merstham. Within a couple of years he was joined by a kinsman, Henry Wood, as curate. In December 1586 the rector officiated at the burial of the infant heir of the main residents, John and Magdalen Southcote, in the knowledge of their Papist persuasion. The Southcotes had inherited Albury and Chaldon manors having offered £40 out of their income of £160 a year for relief from further recusancy proceedings, and were in danger of again being indicted for their 'Romanist' religious observance in 1587.

With France so divided as to be powerless to check Spain's increasing might, England finally agreed in August 1585, to intervene on behalf of the Netherlanders, undertaking to maintain an expeditionary force there as long as the war lasted, a very different situation from that of ten years previously. (As Burghley later said: 'the state of the world is marvellously changed, when we true Englishmen have cause, for our own quietness, to wish good success to a French king and a king of Scots'). Before long, rumours of the approaching attempt to bring England under Spanish imperial power, with an invasion bent on accelerating Mary Stuart's accession to the throne, caused stricter measures against suspected Papists. Both Firle Place and Gatton were searched and a seminary priest called Nicholas Smith, alias Phelps, was captured at Lady Copley's house. Apparently he was believed to be related to the Copleys for Margaret, William's eldest sister, was examined at length on the matter. Certainly her cousin, Father Robert Southwell, was active in London at the time and attracting some notice despite, or because of, his gentle character. Lady Catherine was imprisoned briefly while Margaret, not long after this

The memorial to Magdalen Southcote 1560-1597 is in
Waldegrave's church at Borley on the Essex/Suffolk
border. The latin inscription is translated thus:

As dust within this tomb lies Magdalen,
daughter of Waldegrave, Southcott's only spouse.
Chaste, modest and most devoted wife, children she bore;
Firm in faith and generous of heart she lived.
Death was Life's gift to her; Death's gift was life:
The infant life that robbed her of her own.
O brutal Death approaches, Farewell Life.

44

inquisition, married John, eldest son of Robert Gage of Haling, Croydon, and cousin of John Gage of Firle, to whom her aunt Margaret was married. Confusingly both the Firle and Haling branches of the Gage family were now represented by a John and Margaret (née Copley) partnership.

Despite their religion, there had been nothing so far to suggest that the Merstham-connected gentry were involved in treason. The nearest any member of these families came to political action was when Robert, a brother of John Gage of Haling, who 'deeply feeling the tyrannical oppression under which his religion suffered, after some solicitation, was persuaded by his young and accomplished friend, Anthony Babington of Dethick, to join with him and other Catholic gentlemen of family and fortune in a plot, the object of which was the assassination of the Queen and the liberation of Mary of Scotland from her confinement'.[6] He was one of those duly hanged for his part in the conspiracy. The Copley relationship with the Babington plotter was sufficient excuse for Lord Burghley to fill in the Gatton electoral return for 1586 himself. Possibly at royal instigation, a City gentleman was sent to assess young William Copley's position. It was duly reported to the Queen's Secretary on 30th October that he had been found to be 'very tractable, and will be easily won', but nothing further was attempted at this stage. With the execution of Mary Queen of Scots the following February, and the defeat of the Spanish Armada the year after, there was no longer the same urgency to prosecute those of a papist persuasion, though it remained a useful distraction from the economic burden of maintaining forces at sea, in the Netherlands and in Ireland. The executions of two secular priests in Surrey that autumn were the first religious killings in the country since Henry VIII's reign. Apart from the north, Surrey had the highest proportion of regular recusants in the country (elsewhere it was the Puritans rather who were the focus of government disapproval). Even Copley's friend, Sir Henry Weston, Sheriff of the county but who has been described as 'a good example of the numerous class who would have been recusants if they had dared or cared sufficiently for anything but their safety and comfort',[7] had his house searched for a priest. Nor was the locality safe from Puritan assault: In November 1588 the Rector of Merstham, Richard Wood, had the dubious honour of being pilloried as 'Richard Never-be-Good' in the first of the infamous Marprelate tracts, a sort of early *Private Eye* that abused the Episcopal system with a certain pungent wit. The controversy was still raging when Reverend Wood died and may well have influenced Canterbury in the appointment of one of Merstham's most notable rectors. Thomas Ravis was about thirty when he took on the parish in 1591. Unfortunately for the parish, he also took on the living of All Hallows, Barking, and the prebendary of Westminster within a few months, so that once again the parish had to make do with an absent rector. Partly because of his involvement in the very fine translation of the Bible issued under King James, Ravis went on to be Bishop of Gloucester, then London, before his death in 1609.

By the 1590s there were few of Elizabeth's subjects who had known another ruler and despite the plague, famine and economic depression of these later years, few who would wish for another. Arrangements having been made with the young King James VI of Scotland, one might have thought that Catholicism no longer posed the same political threat. Yet the examples of what divided religion had inflicted on France and the Netherlands strongly influenced the English government in its religious intolerance. Equally the example of what price Thomas Copley had been prepared to pay for his religion influenced his whole family. His son-in-law, John Gage of Haling, was found to have concealed a priest called Beesley (one might have thought his wife, Margaret, would have at least learned from her earlier experience), and was 'let off' with life imprisonment, his forfeited estates being let to Charles Howard, the Lord Admiral and son of Lord Howard of Effingham. William Copley, recently married to Magdalen, daughter of Thomas Prideaux, a fellow exile at the Spanish Court, gave every appearance of conformity at Gatton until he slipped abroad, staying in Spain for the remaining decade of this reign. Another of his sisters, Mary, had married de Teviss, one of the Duke of Parma's captains of horse, and is briefly noted in the State Papers as having used her influence to have

English privateers released from the Spanish galleys. Another sister, Ellen, had become the second wife of Richard Stanihurst, Campion's former friend and pupil. Their brother, Anthony, had been in Spanish service in the Netherlands but returned to England, hoping for pardon and employment. He was arrested, however, and imprisoned in the Tower, being released when he had no more information to pass on. He spent the next few years at Roffey with his mother, writing poetry and, according to Topcliffe's report to the Queen, venting his guilt and frustration in sporadic fits: 'He did shoot a gentleman the last summer, and killed an ox with a musket, and in Horsham church threw his dagger at the parish clerk. There liveth not the like, I think in England, for sudden attempts, nor one upon whom I have good grounds to have watchful eyes'. Not surprisingly he was in and out of prison regularly. In 1592 Topcliffe finally caught Copley's cousin, Robert Southwell, and examined him so severely that his father, Richard Southwell, who had remarried in 1589 and was now residing in Norfolk, was moved to petition the Queen for him to be brought to trial and executed rather than stay in his present filthy hole. As a result he spent two and half years in the relative comfort of the Tower where he provided some support to his fellow prisoner for his faith, Philip Howard, whose grandfather had been brought to the block by his grandfather! He also wrote poetry of a high standard, mainly about spiritual love. The Cambridge History of English Literature states that it is 'practically certain that Shakespeare had read and imitated Southwell'. Adversity is probably a prerequisite for artistry: Certainly Donne, Milton and Shelley were also of recusant stock.

The last few years of Elizabeth's reign were characterised by the rivalry between Robert Cecil (Burghley's younger son) and Robert Devereaux, Earl of Essex, the latter taking the more modern role of leader of the opposition until his execution in 1601. That Merstham was spared the cost of their patronage is partly due to the local influence of the strongly independent Howards of Effingham, and partly to the necessary low profile of its Catholic gentry. Once Robert Southwell was executed for his faith in the spring of 1595, it is not surprising to find the Jesuit Colleges abroad

Robert Southwell 1561-1595
Son of Bridget, née Copley of Gatton, nephew of
Sir Robert Southwell, Merstham's owner. A
contemporary of Shakespeare, he was a Jesuit priest
and poet of some renown.

The lopped tree in time may grow again;
Most naked plants renew both fruit and flower;
The sorriest wight may find release of pain,
The driest soul suck in some moistening shower;
Times go by turns and chances change by course,
From foul to fair, from better hap to worse.

The sea of fortune doth now ever flow,
She draws her favours to the lowest ebb;
Her tide hath equal times to come and go,
Her loom doth weave the fine and coarsest web;
No joy so great but runneth to an end,
No hap so hard but may in time amend.

(Courtesy of The National Portrait Gallery)

48

soon including Copley's, Southwells and Southcotts among their numbers. Robert's father, Richard Southwell, had come under suspicion for his appeal on behalf of his son and was a prisoner in the Fleet prison until his death there in 1600. Henry Garnett, who had been Richard's son's companion when they re-entered England as priests, wrote that July that he died a Catholic. Yet there was division even amongst Catholics, between the minority Jesuit faction who would make no compromise, and the greater number (about 400 in England by now) of secular priests who hoped for some arrangement with the government. Anthony Copley, adopting his usual contrary stance, took the part of the seculars, writing a number of papers, such as *An answer to a letter of a Jesuited gentleman by his Cosin, Maister A.C., concerning the Appeale, State, Jesuits.* His own younger brother, John Copley, was ordained a Jesuit the year after this was published.

When Queen Elizabeth died in March 1603 she left King James of Scotland the increasing financial burden of her government and the aspirations, and frustrations, of all those who had focused on the late Earl of Essex as an unofficial leader of the opposition. Among those hoping for a change were the English Catholic exiles some of whom were able to return in anticipation of the peace treaty with Spain. William Copley was permitted to redeem his estates for £2,000 with an annual levy of £240 thereafter. Merstham's locals cannot have known stranger times than to have a Scottish king, a Danish queen and Spanish-speaking and-behaving children of the returned lord of the manor. The protagonists of the seculars felt sufficiently aggrieved in failing to secure King James' interest in their cause that they plotted to replace him with Lady Arabella Stuart. It would appear that this hopeless plot was betrayed by Henry Garnet and some of his fellow Jesuits. The secular priests involved were executed that December but both laymen involved, Sir Griffin Markham and Anthony Copley, were surprisingly pardoned for their treason, the latter on 18th August 1604. The suspicion that the king intended to become a Catholic (as had Henry IV of France) led to the government's rush to enforce the recusancy fines that November. The main variation in enforcement of the fines was caused by the use of recusants' forfeitures as a form of patronage, but since the property was often granted before the recusant's conviction, this measure gave a number of private individuals an interest in securing such convictions. Certainly wealthy William Copley, with his Spanish relatives, one brother convicted for treason and another a Jesuit, was a prime target.

In anticipation of this, he conveyed his Merstham estates to Nicholas Jordan and John Middleton, both men of insufficient stature to leave any other trace of their existence (they may have been junior members of the Jordans of Gatwick and the Middletons of Charlewood). One is left with a sneaking suspicion that the conveyance was to put the property beyond the grasp of predators and that this may have been some temporary arrangement with two loyal retainers from the Roffey estates. Of the local potential purchasers, the Southcotes of Albury suffered from the same vulnerability of being recusants (and their finances were sufficiently stretched that within three years they had to sell their Leigham Court estate in Tooting to Sir Matthew Carew of Wallington), while the Bests of Alderstead probably could not afford it given both the wool glut and the growth of their families. The parish register of this period is filled with the annual baptisms of Nicholas and Thomas Best's children, almost all daughters. Equally the Howards of Effingham were distracted at the time by the marriage of the sixty-eight-year-old Lord High Admiral to Margaret Stuart, daughter of the Earl of Murray. The Copley's must have expected to be able to maintain their local authority in relative tranquillity until the Gunpowder plot of the following year finally put paid to the aspirations of the recusants. Within months Merstham was sold to John Hedge of Mitcham, whose tenure was fully independent of his Copley neighbours as he also had to buy out both Lady Catherine Copley's life interest, and the £30 annual annuity previously due to Anthony Copley, but forfeited to the Crown on his conviction for treason.

4

REGICIDE AND ROYALIST
1605-1655

Just as Surrey and Sussex generally had a high profile in Tudor times through the eminence of the Howards, so Merstham and Gatton were noted for their Copley connections. Yet neither county nor village were represented by men of similar stature in the subsequent forty years. Of this period it has been said that throughout the country no industrial, agricultural or social change of importance took place while Parliamentary and Puritan Revolution was germinating beneath the soil of an apparently stable and settled society. It was the golden age of the small squire and the yeoman, who prided themselves on their political independence. Personal opinions on Church and State were strongly held in a society composed of small masters whose sense of security denied the old families their former feudal groupings. Merstham's gentry seemed typical of the period.

The christening of Edward Hedge at St Katharine's by Merstham's latest rector, Charles Sonnibanke, testifies to John Hedge being a resident lord of the manor.[5] With the Bests still at Alderstead farm (and Court Lodge, Nutfield) and the Southcotes at Albury manor, he probably made his home at Chilberton manor house in the centre of the village. The building still exists, though substantially altered, as The Manor House in Quality Street. Apart from St Katharine's, Alderstead Farm and the Old Forge, this house and ones either side (North Cottage and Wisteria Cottage) are the oldest surviving structures in the village. Indeed, together with the bland entries of the parish register, these are all that is left to recall Merstham's early Stuart period.

On the evidence available those gentry with status were not necessarily the most established: Unlike the well-rooted and productive Bests, John Hedge the newcomer is referred to as a "gentleman". But senior to him, albeit his tenant, is "Sir" John Southcote, as he was referred to, reinforcing the superiority of the Albury manor. Already a widower and a grandfather (his son, Edward, had married Elizabeth, daughter of John Seaburne of Sutton Court, Herefordshire), John Southcote remained attentive to his family and estate, being much respected locally. Their neighbours, the Copleys, found it more difficult to re-establish a similar position.

William Copley of Gatton now had to run the Roffey estate following the death both of his brother Anthony after a visit to Rome in 1607, and of his mother Lady Catherine Copley in 1608. In 1610 he sent his two daughters, Mary and Helen, abroad. They had some difficulty in their departure. Acting on a tip-off, a justice of the peace with a number of men visited the girls at midnight at the Southwark inn in which they were staying prior to taking ship. The magistrate sat on the bed in which Mary had hid her money for the passage and "demanded the cause of their coming to London, finding nothing against her but her constant resolution not to go to church, asked of the younger if she was also of the same mind, who answered, Yea. Then he willed them to stay in that inn till they heard further from him . . . but in respect of their father being well known there, he did not send them to prison, and so departed. After this they sent their mother word, who lived but fourteen miles off, what had happened; who came speedily up and speaking with the justice got them freed". William still had "one manor and many houses" in South-wark at the time. Sir William Lane, aunt Katherine's progeny, petitioned for the confiscation of, and some benefit from, his recusant relative's property in 1611. He was awarded £160 a year out of the Gatton estate together with

Copley's Southwark Estate circa 1600

£50 for his expenses in prosecuting the same. The attraction of a young lady called Rebecca Moone, rather than this continuing penalisation of the family, may well be the reason for young John Copley's decision to leave the Jesuits for the Anglican Church that year. After four years in the Kentish living of Bethenden he was appointed in 1616 by the Puritan-inclined Archbishop Abbot (who also appointed Thomas Goad to Merstham) to neighbouring Pluckley where there soon developed a constant feud between him and the local squire, Sir Edward Dering, a definite Puritan. Nothwithstanding his uncle's change of heart, William's eldest son, Thomas Copley, had joined the Jesuits and was ordained about 1615, renouncing his rights to his father's estates to his brother, also called William. William the elder requested, and received, naturalisation for his second son, William the younger, who had been born outside England, and set up settlements in his favour. Within three years the new heir had found a bride, Ann Denton, niece of Mary and William Shelton of Ongar Park, Essex, by whom she had been adopted and thus also bore their name.

The following year, 1619, opened with the death outside the parish of Merstham's owner, John Hedge. The estate passed to his son Anthony who within months married one Margaret Fountayne. There is, however, no evidence that they lived in the manor. Coincidentally the lady of the neighbouring estate, Magdalen Copley, died on 30th August, being followed to the Gatton graveyard four months later by her new born son (John). Her husband William was fifty-four years old and preferred to follow the example of Reigate's eighty-four-year-old Lord Howard with his youthful new wife, rather than Merstham's sixty-eight-year-old widower, John Southcote. So Copley too married again, to Margaret, daughter of William Fromonde of Cheam (another known recusant family). It was just as well, for the planned succession went amiss when the heir from his first marriage, William the younger, died a few years later, in his late twenties leaving a widow with two baby girls. Of the other surviving Copley's of Gatton, brother John was vicar of Pluckley, the eldest son Thomas the Jesuit was surreptitiously active in London, and the daughters Mary and Helen were nuns in a convent abroad. The Copley's right to nominate two members of Parliament became less absolute at this time. The franchise only extended to male landowners and six of the seven Gatton households were Copley's tenants in 1620. Yet somehow the "borough" became split into two spheres of patronage. Samuel Oldfield (or Owfield as he then spelt it), having used one of the two seats in 1623, purchased the Chipstead estate from the Bests the following year and established "Upper Gatton" at his manorial court. His was another Lincolnshire family made good in London, and despite his rare local residence, his return for the next three Parliaments established Upper Gatton's right to one of the Gatton seats.

The neighbouring recusant families were not dissimilar. Edward Southcote brought up his family at Albury in the shadow of his father, Sir John's "children, servants and grand-children living in great observance of him". One daughter, Magdalen, spent some time with her Walder-grave aunt, Lady Petre, while the second son, John, was a secular priest and Doctor of Divinity from Louvain, "a great scholar and a fine gentleman". Just as Father Thomas Copley was busy in London, so too was Dr John Southcote as a member and close supporter of the Catholic Bishop Richard Smith. In August 1625 Dr Southcote fell dangerously ill on his way to Ascott House, and spent almost a year recovering, possibly at Albury. His *Notebook* chronicling the London events 1622-37 survive in the archives of the Bishop of Southwark.[8] The activities of the ordained members of that generation of each family left more to posterity than ever anything done by their lay brothers and sisters.

The accession of Charles I brought more change to Gatton than Merstham. Captain Henry Lane, son of Sir William, soon followed his father's example and petitioned for a lease of Gatton in 1630. This was refused, possibly through the influence of Reigate's latest peer. For, after the death of Howard the Lord High Admiral, his widow had married in 1625 her former page, Sir William Monson, whose father was one of the last surviving of Queen Elizabeth's famous admirals. The Monsons were a Lincoln-

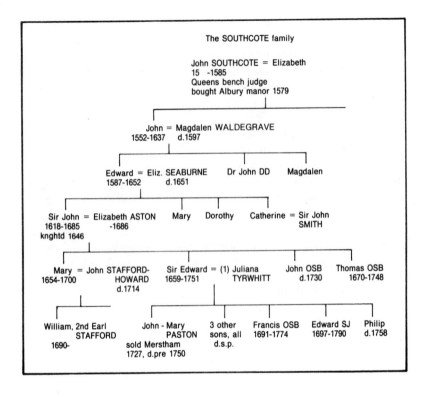

The SOUTHCOTE family

John SOUTHCOTE = Elizabeth
15 -1585
Queens bench judge
bought Albury manor 1579

John = Magdalen WALDEGRAVE
1552-1637   d.1597

Edward = Eliz. SEABURNE   Dr John DD   Magdalen
1587-1652   d.1651

Sir John = Elizabeth ASTON   Mary   Dorothy   Catherine = Sir John
1618-1685   -1686   SMITH
knghtd 1646

Mary = John STAFFORD-   Sir Edward = (1) Juliana   John OSB   Thomas OSB
1654-1700   HOWARD   1659-1751   TYRWHITT   d.1730   1670-1748
                d.1714

William, 2nd Earl   John - Mary   3 other   Francis OSB   Edward SJ   Philip
    STAFFORD   PASTON   sons, all   1691-1774   1697-1790   d.1758
                        sold Merstham   d.s.p.
1690-   1727, d.pre 1750

shire family that had gone on to secure positions of
influence at King James' court, surviving the Thomas
Overbury affair, and whose latest generation were much in
favour with King Charles. Both William and his cousin
John had been knighted (in 1622 and 1625 respectively)
and in 1628 the twenty-one-year-old Sir William was raised
to the Irish peerage as Viscount Monson of Castlemaine. He
still resided with his elderly wife at her Reigate property,
records from which make it clear that his manner was
resented by his local tenants. As a young member of the
Howard household at Reigate, he may well have been a
friend as well as neighbour of the late William Copley the
younger. His own elder brother John was a Catholic
through his marriage to Ann Mayne, and lived not far away
at Kinnersley in Horley, their father's retreat from the sea.
This, together with the knowledge of the King's Catholic
sympathies, suggests Monson was the likely influence in
securing for William Copley in 1632 a pardon for his
recusancy, permitting him secure tenancy of his estates from
the Crown, for the first time for twenty-one years. The same
year Margaret Copley produced a son and heir, Roger, who
was christened at Gatton.

Alternatively the gracious behaviour of the monarch may
have been no more than one of his many methods of raising
funds without having to go to Parliament. For the following
year the Southcote's, of whom there is no record of a prior
sequestration, were re-granted their Albury manor and
other estates at a yearly rent of £100. John Southcote did
not live much beyond this, dying aged eighty-five in 1637.
He was buried at Witham in the vault he had made for his
father, the judge. Of his two sons, Edward was fifty when he
inherited the estates; John was a priest and teacher of
Divinity at Louvain. Edward and Elizabeth had a son,
called John, who was in his early teens and being educated
abroad at the time, and three daughters, Mary, Dorothy
and Catherine.

Over the following ten years, while the King ruled
without Parliament, the Merstham locals adjusted to the
stagnation in trade. In London the opportunities in the
New World were much discussed. Here Father Thomas
Copley had become involved with Sir George Calvert, later

Lord Baltimore, in his Maryland colonisation venture. Copley stayed in London putting heat and spirit of action into the business until 1637 when he himself sailed to the new colony to give personal direction to its foundation. Lord Baltimore was not so influenced by Copley as to allow him total freedom of action in Maryland. But, despite their difference of opinion as to the role of the Jesuit mission, the colony's later Toleration Act embodied principles of religious tolerance that have been traced back to the views of Thomas Copley's exiled grandfather (it did not last long: Royal and exclusively Protestant rule came to Maryland in 1692 and interestingly the first such governor was a Sir Lionel Copley, of the Yorkshire branch of the family). Most colonists, though, were of more humble origins. The son of Gatton's parson, Edmund Shove, was one emigrant who did not survive the journey (though a descendant of his was sufficiently mindful of his origins as to request, some 300 years later, a stone from Gatton church to incorporate into his new Colorado College chapel). Perhaps others from Merstham and Gatton were persuaded by the Copley connection that the New World offered more than the Old in this period. The Poor Laws had brought more organisation than relief to those who fell on hard times, but apart from an incident in neighbouring Bletchingley when cattle taken for distress were forceably recovered, there is no indication that it was economic pressures that determined local allegiances in the coming conflict. As elsewhere it was political and religious opinions that were the main divisive elements.

On the outbreak of the civil war Gatton was represented in Parliament by Sir Samuel Oldfield and Thomas Sandys, though for the first time one of the seats had been contested. Copley had put up Sandys with seven other voters but fourteen non-residents who had purchased some land in the area for the purpose, voted for one of the Sanders family. Parliament determined that, despite one of the voters for Sandys being a "recusant convict", his was the legally correct election. Both Gatton members, like virtually all the other Surrey members, including, surprisingly, Lord Monson for Reigate, took Parliament's side against the King, and it is reasonable to assume that most of the locals felt the same way. The county, in common with Kent and Essex, was by now more strongly influenced by London than in Tudor times and from the start remained secure for Parliament. Certainly with no significant Royalist pocket in the area, Surrey avoided the direct effects of the civil war. Generally, the hostilities provided an excuse to seize or destroy Catholic property (Sir Richard Weston, for example, lost his Sutton estate and had to flee to the Netherlands), but there is no record of such in Merstham or Gatton. The Reverend John Copley was declared a "delinquent" and his Pluckley living sequestrated by Parliament. He may have been given accommodation at Roffey by his elder brother. Months later, on 22nd December 1643, William Copley died at Gatton, aged seventy-nine. Widowed Margaret Copley retired to Leigh Place with her eleven-year-old son. One is thus left guessing as to what legal arrangements may have been made for the Presbyterian, William Oldfield, to be "elected" to succeed to his late father's Gatton seat for Parliament.

Edward Southcote would naturally favour the Royalist cause but, surrounded by Parliamentarians, kept a low profile in Merstham, where moated Albury manor house was sufficiently defensible against any small band of undisciplined opportunists, and left his son John to embark on any heroics. This young cavalier had all the joyful bravado of his generation. For example, once when he visited his sister, the wife of Colonel Stanford, he rode his horse up the great staircase of their hall, not dismounting until he reached the supper table. John distinguished himself mainly with the capture of Captain Hall, the Roundhead commander of "Oliver's own Troop" at the first battle of Newbury. His descendants believed he retired after the Battle of Naseby, but he was at Oxford (which was being gallantly defended by Sir Henry Gage of Haling, Margaret Copley's son) towards the end of the war, and was knighted there on 17th February 1646 for his services by the King. It was probably here that he met and made a life-long friend of Walter, second Baron Aston of Forfar, the hero of Lichfield siege. With the King's surrender three months later, the Royalists gave their parole not to bear arms against Parliament and Sir John Southcote returned to

Merstham with a well-deserved reputation for gallantry. He was next found to be "so much into the favour of my Lady Elizabeth Claypole, Oliver [Cromwell]'s daughter, that they kept a continual correspondence", and, having difficulty adjusting to the sedentary life, made a trip to Rome and Paris, where he bought her damask and dress material.

The increasing gulf between Parliament and its army led to a renewal of sporadic hostilities in 1648 with the Presbyterians initially and strangely allied to the Royalists. Early that May men from all over Surrey met at Westminster Hall to petition Parliament for a settlement with the King and an end to "free quartering" of troops in the county. Tempers were high and fighting broke out, the Surrey men being ejected with some loss of life. Surrey was ripe for a rising when on 23rd May Kent rose in arms. Sir Thomas Fairfax, parliamentary commander, gathered his troops to chase the Kentish forces ultimately to Colchester. Given Cromwell and Lambert were otherwise engaged in South Wales and the North, there was an opportunity to call out the southern counties in more effective protest. When Horsham declared for the King in June, the Earl of Holland, the hesitant Royalist commander, moved out of Westminster to bring the war into Surrey for the first, and last, time.

The rendezvous for all those who would support the Royalist cause was to be Banstead Downs, where the usual horse racing was expected to attract a reasonable crowd, but "the country people here made wiser by the suffering of Kent and Essex do not join with them". Certainly Sir John Southcote, like many another former Royalist of some rank, was not about to break his parole, though it could not have been easy to rest idle as the opposing forces converged on the locality. Historians have wondered at the reason for their subsequent advance on Reigate rather than, say, Guildford and its powder works. Lord Monson had fortified his Holmsdale house some years earlier, the civil war providing him with a useful excuse given the illegality of his continuing occupation of Reigate. The estates had reverted on the death of his first wife to the heiress of the Lord Admiral, the countess of Peterborough, who had so far been unable to assert her title to Reigate Priory. Only days before this rising, Parliament had requested Lord Monson to remove his fortifications "so that the enemy may not be encouraged by them to attempt a surprise of the place, as being tenable when possessed".[9] Equally one of the leaders of the Royalist force was Henry, Earl of Peterborough, the dispossessed countess' son, who may well have wished to settle a personal score. On 7th July the Parliamentary Committee reported to Colonel Rich that the enemy forces were the previous night at Dorking numbering 500 or 600 horse but no foot. "The forces which we have in readiness to meet them are two troops of your regiment of horse, that of Major Gibbons, and 700 horse and foot with Sir Michael Levesey [recently successful at Horsham]". Before this was written the Royalist forces had already occupied Reigate and unsuccessfully skirmished with Major Lewis Audeley's patrol, on detachment from the main Sevenoaks force, in the Battle Bridge area between Merstham and Red Hill. That evening the Royalists evacuated Reigate as Major Gibbons' force advanced via Merstham to Red Hill where, on 7th July, they joined forces with Levesey's troops from the south and chased the Earl of Holland back to Kingston and beyond. Within days unscrupulous Monson had to be reprimanded by Parliament for his premature sequestration of suspect Reigate locals' property. He was also again told to make indefensible his "castle of Holmsdale", which was "garrisoned at the charge of the county whereby the people are much discontented and their dissatisfaction increased".

Although Sir John Southcote had played no part in this campaign, the family's unattended Witham estate was "severely plundered just after the surrender of Colchester by a party commanded by Captain Foster, who left neither lock, latch nor bolt upon any of the doors, nor a whole pane of glass in the windows, and also destroyed all the old writings that were evidence of this estate"[10]. Thirty-eight years later Captain Foster's son was to regret his father's piece of vandalism.

For the moment dissatisfaction was not confined to the Royalists. Even those such as William Oldfield who had staunchly supported Parliament through the war, could not be relied upon when it became a question of establishing a republic, and he was one of those purged from Parliament in December 1648 by Colonel Pride. Lord Monson, on the other hand, was one of the few of the House of Lords remaining to debate the authority on which the King's subjects could try the King for treason. The Lords, mindful of their own precarious position, put on a brave show but the result was inevitable; King Charles I was executed the following month. Once the Royalist cause had been finally destroyed with the uncrowned King Charles II's rout in 1651, Cromwell soon found government through the remaining members of Parliament wanting and, after the distraction of an unnecessary war with the United Netherlands, he established a new Commonwealth Parliament. The first of such Parliaments was called in 1654, without any Peers and excluding such rotten boroughs (controlled by a small concert party of eligible voters) as Gatton and some towns, such as Reigate, being reduced to a single seat, anticipating by some 180 years the Reform Act. Lord Monson, whose peerage was now most unfashionable, played no further part in these affairs.

Yet the "Great Rebellion" of the 17th century was not what would be called a revolution in modern terms. For the great majority there was no interest in widening democracy in anything other than a political sense. The social strata were left largely intact. Unlike Henry VIII's piece of social engineering there were few new gentry and little sudden change in property ownership. One may contrast exiled Copley's position seventy years previously with that of Sir Richard Weston who was able to return and retrieve his estates and was soon busy, with extra resources granted by the Government, on a first English "canal", putting Dutch style locks on the river Wey. Fittingly, perhaps, he also became the powerful guardian of the young Copley girls. Cavalier "malignants" had to pay heavy fines, and authority rested with the Major-Generals rather than the judiciary, but most local gentry continued to operate their estates through the interregnum. On Edward Southcote's death in 1652, Sir John had inherited the Albury, Chaldon and Witham estates without hindrance. He had somewhat more difficulty getting married. In order to impress his much younger bride-to-be, Elizabeth, eldest daughter of his friend Walter, Lord Aston, and granddaughter of the late Richard Weston, Earl of Portland and Charles I's lord high treasurer (no relative, though, to the Westons of Sutton) who lived at Tixall in Staffordshire, he set out from Merstham with "new liveries, six good horses for his coach and five for men to ride with pistols".[10] Half way to the Thames his unlawful troop was arrested and he was released from custody only after his friend Bettie, Cromwell's daughter, went to her father "in a huff" at his intent being so mistaken. She explained how Sir John Southcote "meant him no more hurt than she did, and had only put himself into a handsome equippage going to marry a woman of quality, with intent to settle and live quietly the rest of his life". Southcote was duly married, first by a priest and then by a justice of the peace "according to Oliver's new law", and stayed at Tixall until the birth of his first child, Mary.

The main change to local life was once again religious in origin. Anglican worship had been proscribed and every frenzied enthusiast allowed to preach his own sect. The Englishman's abhorrence of religious zeal stems from this period of Puritan religious "tolerance". Reinforced by local military commanders, ale houses, sporting events and comedy were generally discouraged. In Merstham the remaining church effigies had been buried for safety, that of a medieval Lord Mayor, Nicholas Jamys, not being retrieved until 300 years later. On 1st January 1654 the parish register records the marriage of William Angell, the new "minister" of Merstham, to Barbara Williamson from Westminster. Despite his popularity within the parish, the political nature of his appointment led to his being described some years later by John Aubrey as "the Anabaptist Intruder". That the local hostelries suffered under Major General Barstead's stern rule is evidenced by one Mr Flecknoe, who noted of his 1656 visit that "Merstham is a place where I found nothing to eat for supper but coarse brown bread and butter, a dirty table cloth, and a tankard of beer full of a hundred drowned flies. In the bed a whole warren of starved fleas grazed upon my body — the devil take Merstham!".

Gatton, however, underwent a more permanent change.

Just before his death Sir Richard Weston had married off his two wards, Mary and Anne Copley, to his sons, John and George. The brides were far from willing but their protests were to no avail and their Gatton and Roffey estates became available to bolster the already sizeable Westing holdings. To contribute towards the cost of Sir Richard's expensive experiments in canals, Gatton was sold in 1654. Junior members of the Copley family are recorded as having been buried there over the next forty years, after which the parish was permanently severed from its 200-year connection with the clan. Even the family memorials were removed by subsequent owners. Devoid of all but ghosts, the hamlet then seemed to Aubrey merely "the dormitory of the ancient and gentile family of the Copleys".

5

CITY AND COUNTRY TORY
1656-1704

The new owner of Gatton was, as the first Copley had been, a wealthy London merchant for whom land represented the best available investment. Thomas Turgis was thirty-one years old when he bought Gatton, and other Surrey, Sussex, Hampshire, Middlesex and Warwickshire manors, soon becoming known as one of the wealthiest commoners in England. Unlike the Copleys, the Turgis family stayed in the City, Thomas' wife Mary having City roots, and his sister Elizabeth being married to Henry Tulse, one of his father's apprentices. Thomas' father, of the same name, was a member of the Grocers' livery company and alderman of Vintry ward in the City before his death in 1651. The son thus had an element of inherited wealth but also had the wit to add to it by his own endeavours. He too was a member of the Grocers' Company and one must assume had profited from the effects of civil war on the supply and price of food. Certainly the position of the Grocers' livery company, let alone its members, reached high water mark during this period. In February 1660 it entertained General Monk to a banquet at Grocers' Hall in the city and gave him the freedom of the Company, the first time such an honour had been bestowed. Months later King Charles himself accepted the position of Master of the Company on his state entry to the City.

Thomas' only interest in Gatton was his right to one of its

Parliamentary seats, which he first used in 1659 when Cromwell's successors recalled the old-style Parliament in the period of confusion that led to the restoration of the monarchy. In the excitement generated by the political opportunities offered by a new, cavalier, Parliament, Gatton had another contested election in April 1660. William Oldfield joined Thomas Turgis in a partnership that represented the Upper and Lower Gatton freeholders (which was challenged by Roger James and Robert Wood). Each party received eleven votes, a dead heat. On appeal the election was declared void because the voters were all imported Londoners, but following Charles II's restoration, Turgis was returned, initially with Sir Edward Bowyer the Royalist, and the following year, when the latter secured the county seat, with William Oldfield. It was this Parliament that was responsible for punishing the few surviving regicides available. Lord Monson was fifty-four years old when he lost his title and was sentenced together with Sir Henry Mildmay and Mr Robert Wallop to be drawn in sledges with ropes around their necks from the Tower to Tyburn and back, and thereafter to remain in the Tower for the rest of their lives. Monson spent his last eleven years in close captivity, pondering on the folly of a mis-spent youth. He eventually died in the Fleet prison in 1672. Not for several generations of his royalist cousins was a Monson again to be connected with the Gatton locality.

Once the regicides had been disposed of, there was no proscription of former Roundheads as such. The reaction against the Commonwealth and the Protectorate was limited to the persecution of dissenting Puritans. Parliament represented the wishes of the majority when it imposed uniform conformity on the Anglican Church. From then on (until recently) dissenting sects sought to be allowed to worship separately rather than change the Church of England. The effect on Merstham was minimal. A new rector, Reverend John Harris, was appointed in 1660 and showed his contempt for his commonwealth predecessor by striking out his name in the parish records. But Angell's retirement (to be a school master) was not the wish of his parishoners who held him in some affection. There is little trace of any local dissenters apart from the Catholic Southcotes and a Quaker or two in Gatton and Coulsdon. Ambrose Rigge, a Quaker from Gatton, was imprisoned for twelve months in the Marshalsea gaol for refusing to attend the preaching of Gatton's rector, Robert Pepys, and for teaching children to read, write and cipher, without the bishop's leave! Whilst Puritan cant may not have fitted the new "learned and inquisitive age", it was still too early for religion to be divorced from politics. Indeed whatever religious sympathies that Charles II possessed were with the Roman Catholic faith, so that Catholicism again was to be a significant aspect in the monarch's European aspirations and thus in his relationship with his Government. Over the first decade of the reign a once united royalist Parliament became so disillusioned by the King's Dutch wars, that opposition to the Court ("Tory") party grew in the shape of a Country ("Whig") party.

Most Parliamentary boroughs, though, still had only a few, and wealthy, voters, whereas the City of London enjoyed complete self government on a more democratic basis with some 12,000 voters electing 26 aldermen and 200 Councillors. Here Thomas Turgis concentrated on his City affairs, trading in the growing markets of sugar, tobacco, coffee and tea, and carrying out his livery company tasks. He nominated a number of aldermen from 1659 to 1661, in which year he was himself elected an alderman for the Farringdon Without ward of the City. So busy was he, however, that he preferred to pay the usual fine, of £520, rather than carry out the duties. When William Oldfield died in 1664 leaving his two sons and their stepmother with insufficient authority, Turgis shared his Gatton seat with Sir Nicholas Carew of Beddington Park, Wallington, during this humiliating period of English history. It was bad enough that the Dutch should interrupt City trade without the disruption of both the 1665 Plague when London lost a fifth of its population, and the Great Fire of London the following year, which in five days devoured all the City buildings between the Tower and the Temple. The Grocers' Company, for example, lost all its revenue from rented property, leaving it heavily in debt for decades to come. Yet such was the strength of trade through London that the

City and its individuals did recover and progress. The Stuart assessments make it clear that at that time three quarters of the English population lived south-east of the Gloucester/King's Lynn line. They also chart the rise of Surrey from being the eighteenth richest county in 1636 to be second only to Middlesex in 1693, owing to the expansion of London and its market. Just as the City was expensively rebuilt in brick and stone, so too were a number of Merstham houses (such as 16-22 School Hill, Priors Mead, Wellhead and Hoath Farm) reconstructed of sufficiently sturdy materials to survive to the present day.

Not everyone shared in this prosperity. Generally local landowners of more modest estates, with no outside connections and little income other than from their own farms, began to lose out to the more efficient, capital-intensive, estates. After over 200 years the Best clan, represented only by daughters, had finally lost its identity within the locality. The Alderstead tenancy passed to another local farmer, Joseph Reeve. Equally the Hedge family's property interests are next found to be represented by two married daughters who in 1678 sold Merstham manor to Sir John Southcote. Once more the village had a resident owner, though the change from tenant of Albury manor to lord of Merstham manor made little difference to the status of the Southcotes locally. Elderly Sir John's ability to afford the purchase was no doubt due to the affection his father-in-law, Lord Aston, had for him and Lady Elizabeth. The couple had at least four children at the time, Mary, Edward the heir, John and eight-year-old Thomas (named after the then fourth Earl of Portland). The family regularly spent three or four months each summer at Aston's palatial new Standon estate in Hertfordshire, adjoining the estate of his friend, William Howard, Viscount Stafford.

The Southcotes' connection with the newly-influential Catholic peerage was not, however, the best guarantee of peace and prosperity. The association of Catholicism with Louis XIV's arbitrary form of government, and Charles II's preference to bargain with France rather than his own Parliament for finance, increased the by now traditional fear of Catholicism to levels of frenzied passion in London. Lord Aston had died in April 1678 (his funeral attended by 1,000

Mary and Edward Southcote in about 1664
Devotion to their father's Royalist stance led them to
favour the Jacobite cause. Mary became Lady
Stafford-Howard and Governess to the Prince of Wales.
(Courtesy of Lord Petre)

69

people and his widow so distraught that, according to young Edward Southcote "she grew melanchonly and lost her wits, keeping almost perpetual silence, and refusing nourishment"), being succeeded by his son, Lady Elizabeth Southcote's brother. It was his steward, Dugdale, who, after being dismissed for embezzlement, "made his discovery" of a Popish plot, thus adding credibility to the Titus Oates allegations that charged the national atmosphere with anti-Catholic mania. The exact balance of local feeling is impossible to determine. Southcote's coachman, Will Harrison, was prepared to give evidence in defence of a Jesuit that December, while the whole Southcote family bar the minors, John and Thomas, appeared at the Old Bailey in defence of a further five Jesuit priests in June 1679. Among the Catholic peers committed to the Tower for treason were Lords Stafford, Aston and Petre (whose connection with the Southcotes went back a century to the Waldegrave marriage), so that even in Merstham the position of the Southcotes must have seemed precarious. Certainly the invented plot caused a spate of judicial murders of accused Papists, actual or not, destroyed forever the "Cavalier" parliament and threatened the throne.

It cannot be assumed that the two members for Gatton, Turgis and Carew, were sympathetic to the Whigs simply because they were members of the Exclusionist Parliaments. The "rotten" nature of the captive borough isolated them from becoming prey to sudden changes of political opinion, despite an attempt from Upper Gatton, Sir John Thompson, William Oldfield's brother-in-law, to regain control of one of the seats. The Thompsons were originally from Hertfordshire but had made their fortunes in London. They were strongly Parliamentarian. Whilst Sir John Southcote had earned his knighthood at the battle of Newbury, the Roundhead opposing force with the highest casualties had been commanded by Sir John Thompson's uncle. Sir John Thompson had been a governor of the East India Company during the Commonwealth (which had since become the Whigs' main financing vehicle) and was also known as a powerful friend of the Dissenters. He must have been surprised to fail in replacing Sir Nicholas Carew in the panic election of February 1679. The following year the

Whig frenzy culminated in the execution of the sixty-eight-year-old Lord Stafford, "one of the most disgraceful episodes in the story of the House of Commons", as Disraeli was to describe it. It did, however, provoke a sudden national sympathy for the humiliated King, especially among those with rural Tory opinions. The Royalist reaction of 1681 originated in Oxford but spread rapidly to the Whig London stronghold. That year Sir John Moore, leader of the City's small Tory party and member of the Grocers' company, secured the post of Lord Mayor for 1682 and, by dint of ancient precendent rather than due election, appointed Tory sheriffs to the City. The King followed up this success the following year by issuing a new commission that reappointed eighteen of the existing aldermen, including the next Lord Mayor, Turgis' brother-in-law, Sir Henry Tulse, and replaced eight Whig aldermen with loyal Tories, one of whom was Sir Benjamin Newland. Turgis' political allegiances can now be more easily assumed: His brother-in-law and fellow Grocer was clearly a Tory, and their nephew Edward Turgis had married his two daughters to a Scriveners' partnership, Simon Beckly and George Newland, the latter being son of the loyal Tory, Sir Benjamin Newland. Thus in the City were politics and business united.

The new Tory enthusiasm for the Crown came late to Merstham. In May 1681 Albury Manor was stripped of anything of value by bailiffs acting under instruction from Joseph Reeve, sheriff but also Southcote's tenant for Alderstead manor. He was invoking the Elizabethan recusant laws instigated by Southcote's great-grandfather. Interestingly there remains deep in Merstham quarries both a cunningly hollowed stone for secreting valuables or chaplain's effects, and a rhyme (about the value of patience) enscribed on the wall dated that year. There has been some speculation that this may have served as a temporary refuge for an educated hand to be in evidence there at that time. Despite their opposing views, it was another of Southcote's neighbours, Sir John Thompson, who obtained a *quietus* from the Attorney General on their behalf.

Charles II was now able to carry on without a Parliament. He relied on the Torys' preconcern with the avoidance of rebellion and disorder, rather than religious dissent, to enable the due succession, in February 1685, of his legitimate heir, James, the first Catholic ruler since Mary. That May Gatton returned Thomes Turgis to the new, predominately Tory, Parliament with a different partner, Sir John Thompson who had last tried for the seat at the height of the Whig challenge. It was thus this unlikely partnership that represented Gatton in Parliament's support of the King's suppression of Monmouth's rebellion that year. However, whether for political or for business reasons, Thompson shortly afterwards took his family to the Netherlands, only returning to join Turgis and the rest of Parliament when it moved into opposition to the King as James II increasingly disregarded its advice.

Elderly Sir John Southcote barely survived the succession, dying on 27th May 1685. One is left with the impression that he typified the popular image of the gay cavalier, able to charm friend and foe alike, enjoying life to the full without sacrificing dearly-held principles of faith and loyalty. Traditionally it was the refusal of Reverend James Sambourne, Merstham's rector since 1679, to bury him in the chancel of St Katharine's, that led to his family leaving Albury manor on religious grounds. What makes the Southcote's refusal to accept Sambourne's decision slightly more understandable is that it was only recently that Sir John's Catholic grandfather, the first Earl of Portland, had been buried in Winchester Cathedral, while the vicars of St Nicholas', Witham, were consistently tolerant. Edward Southcote and his mother next hired a house "within three doors of St James' Gate" in the parish of St Martin-in-the-Fields, then in Middlesex. Here, with her brother still a prisoner in the Tower, Lady Southcote arranged the marriage of twenty-eight-year-old Mary to Lord Stafford's younger son, John Stafford Howard, "while Dugdale was drinking himself to death haunted by his unhappy victim's ghost". At the same time she concluded a match between Edward and Juliana, the only daughter of Sir Philip Tyrwhitt. Whilst on her deathbed in January 1686, she charged Edward not to delay the marriage beyond eight days from her burial. Having interred her body in the

Witham family vault, Edward was duly married to Juliana by Bishop Ellis at the fashionable Savoy chapel of Marius Corker (the Stafford's chaplain), Mary Stafford-Howard and her sister-in-law, Isabella, Marchioness of Winchester being among the five attending. The Southcotes stayed in London until their newly reconstructed Witham Place was ready for occupation. From this period Albury manor and Merstham fell into neglect while Witham prospered. Whatever the quarrel between Merstham's rector and squire, there can be no doubt it was to the detriment of the village. For generations, locals were wont to recall that *"during the Southcotes' residence no calamity or casualty happened, no unproductive season occasioned a scarcity, but ready assistance was given"*.[11]

Certainly Merstham's owner had everything to gain from the King's promotion of his Catholic friends. Sir Edward Southcote, whose knighthood apparently dates from this time, was first cousin of the Smiths. John Smith was brother-in-law of Henry, Lord Waldegrave, the husband of the King's favourite natural daughter, Henrietta Fitzjames, while his sister Catherine Smith married the son of the King's banker, Sir Daniel Arthur. Complicated, but it does help explain how and why this generation of Southcotes adopted a less reconciliatory tone politically than its predecessors both generally and locally. Both Sir Edward and the newly released Lord Aston gave evidence against Titus Oates in 1685. Shortly afterwards Sir Edward was appointed Justice of the Peace and Deputy Lieutenant for Essex, in which capacity he "could not forbear smiling" to see Captain Foster's son convicted by his colleagues for sheep stealing in 1687. Then came the Revolution of 1688 and James II fled to France with most of his Catholic Court. Once again, though over one hundred years later, Merstham's owner and JP thought it advisable "to step just to the other side of the water to observe what demands would be made". For, having acted in three commissions without having taken the oaths required under the re-invoked Test Act, Sir Edward was conscious of the potential £1,500 fine. In the event he was back in England within a year as "by good luck so many of the Non-Cons had also acted without taking the oaths, the Government to favour them dropped the prosecution". The rest of the family stayed abroad, Mary because her husband was part of the Court in exile, and the two younger brothers, John and Thomas, having completed their education at Douai, to be ordained into the exiled English Benedictine order there.

Thomas Turgis and Sir John Thompson, meanwhile, had been duly returned to the Convention Parliament that declared William and Mary as King and Queen in return for a Declaration of Rights. William of Orange was in any event more interested in bringing England into his anti-French alliance than in its domestic politics. Turgis continued his low profile Tory role, quietly supportive of the newly-formed Bank of England, tenant of the new Grocers' Hall, in its difficult early years. Sir John Thompson, though, had a higher, Whig, profile and, no doubt building on his Dutch connections, rose to a position of some prominence under the new regime. He was a constant speaker in the Commons, particularly on Free Trade, while promoting his business interests in the campaigns against the French. Otherwise he was best remembered for providing "Great Fire Works", though unfortunately not locally. Indeed the folk of Upper Gatton had little interest in this typical war profiteer. Thompson fitted the description of the emerging landowners of the time "who were peculiarly susceptible to considerations of social prestige and political power. Among them were a few large merchants, mainly chairmen of the East India Company, who went in for politics. They bought up blocks of land in different parts of the country, bought out some of the surrounding gentry, bought advowsons and, in many cases, the manorial rights of Parliamentary Boroughs. They were not so much investing their money in land as buying up the perequisites of a social class, the undisturbed control of the life of a neighbourhood. The hatred of the small squires for the great lords, whether old or new, who were buying them out is the theme of many contemporary plays".[12] Thompson was by no means the last to treat Gatton in this manner. He himself went on to secure a peerage, as Lord Haversham, in 1696 when appointed a Lord of the Admiralty. Having moved to the Upper House he no longer had need of a Commons seat and sold his Upper Gatton interests in 1704.

After Lord Haversham's death in 1710, his vast wealth was totally squandered by his useless son, Samuel.

If the other non-resident member for Gatton, Thomas Turgis, had a son, he must have died without issue before his father. For on Turgis' death in June 1704, "leaving an estate worth over £100,000", Gatton passed to William, eldest son of his niece, Rebecca, and her husband, George Newland. Turgis was buried in St Dionys Backchurch, which used to be in Fenchurch Street, in the City. This prestigious last resting place for an eminent Grocer has no more survived than St Olaves, Tooley Street, the last resting place of the eminent Mercer, Copley. St Andrews church at Gatton, though, remains an elegant shrine to mainly humbler folk.

Sir Edward Southcote was, of course, a generation younger than his Parliamentary neighbours. Despite his obvious Jacobite connections, he had been specifically licensed to return to England, but he still preferred to live at Witham "in an iron cage of double taxes" with his ten children, especially while Reverend Sambourne was still rector at Merstham. Sir Edward's sister, Mary, was governess to the young Prince of Wales for the last six years of her life, dying fifteen months before her monarch, James II, at Saint-Germain. Both Father John and Father Thomas were by then working from the London Mission, the latter being remembered best for bringing the assistance of one friend, Dr Radcliffe of Oxford, to another friend, the young Alexander Pope. Certainly the Southcotes could still wield some influence but Merstham had no more benefit of it now than did Gatton of its owners. In 1704, as Gatton changed hands, Southcote gave the use (but not full title) of most of Merstham over to Henry Hoare, the latest of a local farming family that, according to the parish register, once rivalled the Bests for procreation.

6

TRADERS' REST
1705-1785

The coalition ministry selected by Queen Anne to support the Grand Alliance against Louis XIV was reflected in the continuing division of Gatton's parliamentary seats. Young William Newland had inherited his great-uncle's Gatton estate whilst under age (he was only nineteen) so that the family's Tory interests were represented initially by his father, George Newland, who, having secured his knighthood in June 1706, removed the family from the stench of Smithfield to their new Surrey parkland. In 1704 Lord Haversham had sold Upper Gatton, and Chipstead manor, to a fellow Whig, Paul Docminique, an eminent sixty-one-year-old merchant of Huguenot origin. Paul Docminique's family were from Lille, then part of the Spanish Netherlands, until driven by religious prosecution to England. His proudest boast well into old age was how he remembered seeing Oliver Cromwell going to Parliament House for the last time. He was naturalised in 1662 and married a vicar's daughter, Martha Edwards, twelve years later. As typical an example of the new commercial oligarchy as his colleague, Lord Haversham, he was rewarded for his efforts with the Proprietorship of New Jersey in 1692 (the connection with Lord Haversham is reinforced by an earlier abortive attempt to re-name Westerly, Rhode Island, "Haversham"). It would seem that he moved to Chipstead about the same time that the Newlands moved to Gatton. Merstham, meanwhile, remained squireless. Later, though, the settlement of Chaldon manor by Sir Edward Southcote on his eldest son, John, at the time of his marriage to Mary Paston of Bessingham, Norfolk, in 1709, raised the possibility of a future return of the Jacobite Southcotes to their Surrey property.

Despite Marlborough's impressive defeat of the French, the first defeat that the French army had suffered for over two generations, the English electorate was war-weary and concerned for the Anglican Church under an increasingly Whig-dominated Parliament. By 1710 they reacted by returning one of the largest Tory majorities to date. Paul Docminique kept his captive Upper Gatton seat, while William Newland took over his rightful "Lower" Gatton seat from his father, Sir George, who was more democratically returned for the London seat instead. Then, in April 1713, the villagers of Merstham, Gatton and Chipstead, regardless of the politics of their landlords, joined the rest of the country in celebrating the Peace of Utrecht with bonfires and bells. Such unity was only temporary. As Queen Anne became more seriously ill, tavern gossip centred more on the value of the Act of Settlement. The Queen's preference for her half-brother, the Prince of Wales, to her Hanoverian relatives, was matched in the shires by the preference of many country squires "to see, instead of an aged German princess, the grandson of King Charles the Martyr back in an English palace — provided he would change his religion". Amongst those involved in the complex but abortive negotiations was Father Thomas Southcote whose influence with several senior Tories permitted him relatively easy passage from his Standon base. Amidst all this political frenzy the suicide on 26 March 1714 of Sir George Newland passed virtually unnoticed, and certainly unexplained. He was buried at Gatton. William continued the family Tory tradition, voting with the opposition throughout the next reign.

The accession of George, the Elector of Hanover, to the recently united British throne, was a triumph for the Whigs and their Whimsical Tory allies, Paul Docminique's not insignificant role can be gauged by his rapid appointment on 13th December 1714 to the influential post of Commissioner of the Board of Trade & Plantations. This royal committee governed the relationship between Britain and its colonies, which, in order of then importance, were the West Indies, Newfoundland, India, North America and Africa. Docminique was seventy-one at the time. In an age when patrimony was accepted as being more important than merit it is remarkable that the massive commercial appetite of the nation should have been managed so efficiently by this unelected, eight member oligarchy. Later the extent to which the colonies were controlled by the Crown's executive, and not Parliament, was to give rise to the constitutional issues that led to American independence. But, for now, it allowed continuity of pragmatic administration, unfettered by the vagaries of domestic politics. Paul Docminique was to spend twenty years on the Board, being paid £1,000 per annum for the post, under the presidency of first Henry Howard, sixth Earl of Stafford, and secondly the Earl of Westmorland. In contrast his two sons, Charles and James Docminique, appear to have held no public office.

The new Hanoverian regime was not totally accepted. The Jacobite rebellion of 1715 is best remembered as a Scottish affair, but it had its adherents throughout the realm. Father Thomas Southcote had been continuously involved in the cause of "James III" and "with his skill in slipping in and out of England aboard the ships smuggling wool, known as *owlers*, he was almost first with the news of the escape of Thomas Forster, the Northern leader, from the Essex coast". As a result of this rebellion all Catholic non-jurors were required to register their estates. The result is an interesting testament to the efficacy of Elizabeth I's religious policy. In all Surrey only the Weston's estates (including Colley manor that they had acquired from the Copleys) represented a Catholic holding of any size, and that was four times as large as the next largest. Sir Edward Southcote registered his Witham estate, while his son John registered Chaldon and Albury manors, the latter being valued at £274. Father and son also registered their interests (the one capital, the other revenue) in a Nayton (Drayton?) manor in Berkshire. The register was appropriate; the Jacobite cause remained persistent and fund raising its more obvious need. Father Thomas Southcote was "in some measure master of the avenues of business" on behalf of his King over the water, and was constantly in touch with Jacobite sympathisers in the Tory ranks. He and his brother John drew an annuity from the family's Witham, but not Merstham, estates. In July 1722 the Secretary of State received the following intelligence from Paris: "There is one Sercute, an English Benedictine monk who is to be very speedily despatched as a courier to England; he is much in the confidence of the Jacobites and has distinguished himself in that party by his activity during the last Rebellion, having often thrown off his habit to serve the Cause. I shall endeavour to get him secured, though he is pretty dexterous. I am told he is a brother of Sir Edward Sercute, of a good family in England". Plots and arrests abounded but Father Thomas remained at liberty while Father John left his work in the south of England, retiring to St Edmund's, Paris where he stayed until his death in 1730.

Locally the area was isolated from the events of the period. If it suffered from the increasing drift of population, evident elsewhere in the home counties, from rural poverty to the opportunities of the gin-and-pox-ridden City, it is not obvious from the parish registers. When Reverend James Sambourne died in 1723, the parish reverted to having a less resident rector, Reverend Henry Mills being also chaplain to the Whitgift hospital in Croydon. Bearing in mind the cause of the quarrel between Sambourne and the Southcotes, and the effect on the village over the last forty years, it is interesting that he too was not buried in St Katharine's chancel, unlike his predecessor and successor rectors. Perhaps the parish determined it so. Furthermore, at a time when people were still being executed for witchcraft in provincial England, Mr Sambourne had been said to possess supernatural powers: Noticing a would-be pear thief in the Rectory orchard, he "fixed his gaze upon the robber from a suitable distance and from where he stood, using dreadful arts, fastened the robber in the tree"![13]

It is possible that John Southcote lost out from the South Sea Bubble as he is next found living in Dunkirk, abandoned by his wife, Mary, who went to live with relatives at Bures Hall on the Suffolk/Essex border. In 1727 Sir Edward, now a widower of sixty-eight, came to his eldest son's rescue by settling on him the Witham estates, having himself negotiated a suitably remunerative second marriage. His brother, Father Thomas, through his friendship with Alexander Pope, had secured Walpole's influence with the French Court which was of considerable help in being appointed abbot of a wealthy Avignon abbey that same year. Equally his other sons were by now either ordained priests or otherwise self-sufficient. The Witham transfer thus allowed John Southcote to realise some much-needed cash by selling his Merstham properties and, in doing so, finally relinquished the family's 148-year connection with the village. The necessary Act of Parliament for the property transfer is informative:

Albury manor house (" The Place")	*30 acres*
Albury farm (£20 rent)	*37 acres*
Chaldon farm (£90 rent)	*407 acres*
Dean farm (£30 5/- rent)	*134 acres*
Goings & Crabfields (£60 rent)	*95 acres*
Hoare's Farm	*21 acres*
Buckner's farm	*10 acres*
Spraborough's farm	*5 acres*

The purchaser of these and other parts of the estate was their octogenarian neighbour, Paul Docminique of Chipstead. This change of ownership did nothing to relieve Merstham of its poor economic condition though. The lack of building and brevity of parish records for the period confirm the impression given to later chroniclers that the early Georgian era represented a low point in the village's fortunes.

Paul Docminique was ninety-two when he died on 17th March 1735. Right to the last he had been a regular attender of the Board of Trade and the Houses of Parliament. He had "represented" his Gatton seat for thirty years and was one of the few remaining members to pre-date the Act of Union. He was succeeded by his surviving son, Charles, who, either through apathy, or antipathy to

Walpole, was only once recorded as having voted. Shortly afterwards the other Gatton seat changed hands following the death of fifty-three-year-old William Newland on 4th May 1738. He was succeeded by his younger brother, George, rather than his three married daughters. George was then vice president of Magdalen College, Oxford, and professor of geometry for Gresham College, London. In connection with the latter position a rival academic said "it is a genteel sinecure, and no wonder a learned man did not get it, the citizens of London being friends of little else but Trade". George Newland continued the family's Tory tradition by voting with the opposition on every occasion. Lord Egmont described him as "a strong Jacobite", which is more likely to mean he represented the extreme views of a party that had been out of office for forty years, than he was a committed follower of the Pretender.

The rebellion of 1745 was mainly a Scottish affair, without even the involvement of the Southcotes to make it pertinent to the locality. Of more interest locally was the appointment of the new rector. The previous incumbent, Reverend Thomas Tanner had moved on to a Suffolk position after less than two years in the parish. The new rector was the Archbishop of Canterbury's newly married son-in-law, Reverend Jeremiah Milles, better known for his antiquarian than for his theological interests. Educated at the expense of his uncle, the Bishop of Waterford & Lismore, Milles had made an extensive Grand Tour of Europe with his cousin, the future bishop of Meath, from 1733 to 1737 and impressed a select but appreciative audience with his observations. He then entered the Church and was employed in his uncle's Irish bishopric until the latter's death in 1740, when the resultant "considerable fortune" permitted him to look for a more appropriate English living. Through the Archbishop's favour he had already secured the sinecure rectory of West Tarring in Sussex and been collated to the rectory of Saltwood with Hythe in Kent, before additionally being appointed to Merstham. Within a year he was to relinquish his Kentish living in favour of the wealthy parish of St Edmund the King, Lombard Street, in the heart of the City.

When Charles Docminique died in 1745 "of a mortification of his foot", his large estate passed to his cousin, Paul Humphrey, whom Lord Egmont was to describe as "a very low odd man". When Humphrey's partner for Gatton, George Newland, died on 22nd October 1749, he quickly took the opportunity to offer the other Gatton seat to the best bidder. His eventual nomination went to a man whose connection with Gatton is only incidental but whose character is of sufficient interest to merit inclusion: Rear-Admiral Sir Charles Knowles was a larger-than-life Hornblower, though with fewer scruples. He had joined the navy at fourteen, rising rapidly to be the commander-in-chief of the Jamaica squadron in 1747 at forty-three. Despite his plea to the Admiralty that he had "more the glory of his Majesty's arms at heart than views after private lucre", he and the then governor of Jamaica used their posts to secure personal privileges in trading with the captured French colonies to the exclusion of other local merchants. He was ordered in 1749 to be court-martialled on charges of negligence in the previous year's action against the Spanish Havana squadron, the last action of the war of the Austrian Succession, as it turned out. With an electorate of only twenty-two voters, Knowles succeeded by one vote, a situation only made possible by the independence of the "Lower" Gatton voters from Humphrey. Otherwise voters in a rotten borough ran the risk, common at the time, of having their house demolished if they failed to exercise their vote according to their landlord's wishes. Another naval officer was told that "the cunning admiral has got a seat in the House of Commons last week, and it is supposed he will have art enough to acquit himself at his trial". The admiral pleaded that news of the end of the war had prevented him from following up the indecisive engagement, and he escaped with a reprimand. He gave up his Gatton seat when, in 1752, he secured the lucrative governorship of Jamaica.

It was an age when many a squire's son was attracted to fight for a fortune in a foreign land. James Wolfe had left Westerham for an army commission at only fourteen, while Robert Clive was twenty-seven when he established a European reputation at the siege of Arcot. Merstham was bereft of such families. Indeed so dilapidated had Albury's moated manor house become that it was pulled down in 1750. Curiously some of its stone armorial work found its way into St Katharine's. A beam was used in the rebuilding of Wellhead Cottage at the time. Otherwise nothing now remains locally of the once respected Southcote family. Coincidentally ninety-three-year-old Sir Edward Southcote died the following year, predeceased by his eldest son. Paul Humphrey also died in 1751, leaving his Chipstead and Merstham estates to his sixty-eight-year-old sister, Rachel. Her recent second husband, Reverend John Tattershall, the Chipstead rector's son was some thirty years her junior. Newland's heirs, meanwhile, through an Act of Parliament, finally secured the sale of the Gatton estate, ending in this case, a Tory family connection that went back ninety-five years to when Thomas Turgis had first bought the Parliamentary seat.

It was precisely the value of this rotten "borough", rather than any reflection of the worth of "the manor and mansion house of Gatton, and advowson, and the manor and farm of Lichfield in Reigate and Gatton, with diverse farms" that attracted James Colebrooke to pay £23,000 for the estate in November 1751. He also purchased the Alderstead manor from a Samuel Nicholson. His father had established a banking partnership, Colebrooke & Lightfoot, at the Royal Exchange in the City, which profited as an army contractor and as an underwriter of war loans. James was the second of three sons. His elder brother, Robert, having generously persuaded the voters of Maldon to elect him to Parliament ten years earlier, had since become such a spendthrift that, when his father died in 1752, it was thirty-year-old James not Robert, that took over as head of the family banking business. He had no trouble with his Tattershall neighbours in re-establishing his right to one of the Gatton seats in the 1754 election; the Tattershalls were sufficiently indebted to the Duke of Bedford, to let him control the nomination of their Gatton seat. With James Colebrooke's younger brother, George, taking over the family seat of Arundel that year, all three Colebrooke brothers were now members of Parliament, a position they held for the next seven years.

As independent Whigs, the Colebrookes would have been

interested more in the influence of the office than the policy of the party, so that the machinations of Newcastle and Pitt the elder were secondary to the possibility of securing valuable contracts when war with France, the Seven Years War, broke out in earnest in 1756. From disastrous defeat Pitt led the country to sublime success, effectively destroying France's ability to compete commercially throughout the trading world. From 1760 the City became increasingly enriched from flourishing new trades and industry so that even the new level of taxation, taking up to fifteen per cent of a landowner's income, was affordable in the new shared prosperity. The growth in vehicular traffic had already prompted the better maintained, self-financing (when the trustees were honest) turnpike roads and one such linked Reigate with Sutton. As this new road increased the traffic between Merstham and Reigate Hill, Colebrooke got authority to close the Pilgrims Way that ran through Gatton, replacing it with a new road, now known as Gatton Bottom, on his northern boundary. Gatton's rectory was then moved to Tower Lodge. The landscaping of Upper and Lower Gatton, reputedly by "Capability" Brown, took place at this time, Gatton lake being formed out of the former glebe. In 1759 James acquired a baronetcy, of Gatton, the first time a hereditary title had been associated with the borough since Philip of Spain had honoured Copley. When Sir James suddenly died aged thirty-nine in 1761, his younger brother, George, took over the family title and estates (Robert had fled abroad to escape his creditors). Sir George Colebrooke was described as a "pretty little dapper man when at his best". As he was already MP for Arundel, he duly returned Colonel Edward Harvey, the brother of a friend of his, for Gatton. Apart from his banking interests Colebrooke was senior in the Honourable East India Company, being elected a director in 1767. He was thus a powerful ally of the new class of *nabobs*, who, "laden with the spoils of Indian service, were buying their way at all costs into the House of Commons, and eclipsing the ancient splendour of the highest and wealthiest county lords".

The other lasting monument to the Colebrookes, and to the sense of humour of Sir George in particular, was the erection in 1765 of a cast-iron Doric Temple to act as a

Gatton's 'Town Hall' built in cast iron by Sir George
Colebrooke in 1765

"Town Hall" for this rotten borough's "elections". It is
possible that the accompanying classical voting urn was
added later when Colebrooke found himself the butt of
popular envy. Pevsner, whilst noting it a very English
political joke, also reflects that the Latin inscriptions, "The
well-being of the people is the supreme law. The lot drawn,
the urn remains. Let evil deception depart", are in keeping
with the melancholic Romantic reaction of Gray's *Elegy* and
Goldsmith's *Deserted Village*. This cynicism was especially
appropriate to the next election in 1768 when Colebrooke's
nominee was a fellow banker, Joseph Martin of Bookham,
and the Tattershall/Bedford nominee was John Damer,

Extract from J Roques' Map 1768

86

Lord Milton's eldest son, who was a typical profligate rake of the period. Eight years later, when his father finally refused to extricate him from his debts, Damer determined to go out in style. He committed suicide after a night of wine, women and song, — or, to be more exact, after a supper *etc* in Covent Garden with "four common women and a blind fiddler"!

The 1763 peace treaty had restored to France some of her losses, but the villagers of Merstham were still assured an abundant supply of tea from India, sweetened with sugar from the West Indies, at a price that made it an economic as much as a moral alternative to spirits and beers. "Any person who will give himself the trouble of stepping into the cottages of Surrey at meal times, will find that in poor families, tea is not only the usual beverage in the morning and evening, but is generally drank in large quantities at dinner".[14] A significant proportion of such imported "necessities" was smuggled to avoid the excise duty, various routes from the Kent and Sussex coasts to London being used by such men as "the Godstone pirate". The old East/West Pilgrim's Way had long since been superceded by more efficient coastal navigation. Significantly the increase in Merstham's buildings, and rebuilding, evident from this time, is mainly North/South along the High Street, reflecting the increasing use of the then Reigate to Croydon route which ran along Linkfield Lane to Battle Bridge Farm on Wiggey Street (now Frenches Road), up School Hill and Quality Street (then both part of the village High Street) and on past Marling Glen (which is believed to have been built as a pub at that time) over Merstham Hill. In particular the Rectory was rebuilt by Jeremiah Milles in the Palladian style in 1768, and remains, as Pevsner calls it, the "*beau ideal* of the comfortable C18 parson's home".

For almost as long as he had been Rector of Merstham, Milles had also held the precentorship of Exeter cathedral with the emoluments of a canon extraordinary, until he became Dean of Exeter in 1762. He also had a strong interest in Devonshire history, so that it is likely he attended his Exeter, rather than Merstham, duties until the completion of the new Rectory. His appointment as President of the Society of Antiquaries in 1768 may well be the cause of his return to a parish more convenient for this new role, but it was an unfortunate coincidence that the antique painted glass in St Katharine's should have "vanished" whilst he was there. Merstham's new owner, Reverend James Tattershall, who had inherited the Docminique estates from his late brother in 1769, was rector of Streatham and St Paul's, Covent Garden, as well as political agent to the Duke of Bedford, and so clearly had little interest in the affairs of Merstham. When Milles died, in 1784, he was buried in his prestigious City parish of St Edmund's rather than at St Katharine's Merstham. His family memorials are virtually the only ones in that Lombard Street interloper edifice.

In 1769 Sir George Colebrooke of Gatton was elected Chairman of the East India Company at a critical stage of its long history. Lord Clive had recently returned from India and added Claremont (Esher) to his estates for £25,000. Apart from their involvement with "John Company", both men were in their mid-forties, MPs, and of course wealthy. Whatever their past differences of opinion, the two families got on well at this time and it may well be through the Colebrookes that Clive employed Capability Brown to rebuild Claremont's house and gardens. Perhaps it was Clive's influence that led Colebrooke, hitherto a prudent banker, to speculate in commodities. In 1771 he bought estates in Lanarkshire for their lead mining potential, added plantations in Grenada and Dominica to those in Antigua already inherited by his wife, and was still able to afford a dealing loss of £190,000 in the flax market! The following year he tried to corner the world supply of alum, purchasing in the process the alum mines in Lancashire and Yorkshire. He helped finance this through broking in East India Company stock, even then not strictly permissible for an officer of the company, let alone its chairman. Meanwhile the worst famine Bengal has ever known, coupled with greedy mismanagement, left "John Company" worse off than its merchant officers. Colebrooke appointed Warren Hastings to the governership of Bengal to reform the administration, but already the political vultures were gathering. Apart from the Select Committee's enquiries which almost halved the Company's stock value, Colebrooke suffered a further loss through his banking firm's exposure

Sir George Colebrooke in the centre, Clive standing on
the right. A satirical print from the *Town and Country
Magazine*, 1773

to the collapse of the Scottish banker, Alexander Fordyce,
in 1772. As a deliberate confidence-boosting show of
affluence he restored St Andrew's church though it failed to
impress those steeped in the politics of envy, for whom it
was "an expiatory step for the hecatombs of human
offerings sacrificed by his friends in India to the God of
Avarice", according to *The Craftsman*. Colebrooke's bank
suspended business at the end of March 1773, and George
did not seek re-election to the East India Company board.
In any event Lord North's India Bill went before the House
that year and Colebrooke, the Whig proponent of self-
regulation, had to accept the Company being subjugated to
Tory statutory regulation. He had to sell most of his
property to satisfy his creditors: On 9th January 1774 the
Annual Register notes "Sir William Mayne, Bart. has
purchased Gatton, in Surrey, the seat of Sir George
Colebrooke, together with the borough, for the sum of
£75,000". The Colebrookes had made a magnificent
country seat out of Gatton in the two decades since they
bought it for £23,000. Sir George had brought up his

family there. In particular his third son, Henry Thomas Colebrooke, the eminent Orientalist, spent his formative years at Gatton, steeped in classics and mathematics. Thereafter the family seat of the Gatton baronetcy was to be at Colebrooke Park, north east of fashionable Tunbridge Wells.

Sir William Mayne was one of twenty-one children of Mayne of Clackmannan, near Stirling, who together with a brother or two operated a banking partnership from Jermyn Street, London. Having spent his early years representing the Lisbon end of the business, William returned to Britain in 1751, and within six years he had become a director of the Royal Exchange Assurance Company, one of only two chartered companies, established after the South Sea Bubble, to successfully compete with the private insurance firms operating out of Lloyd's coffee house. In 1758, aged thirty-six, William married Frances, daughter of Viscount Allen, through whom he acquired considerable estates in Ireland. In 1760 he took the Carysfort seat in the Irish Parliament and was shortly awarded a baronetcy for his adherence to the Whigs at a time when the local imported establishment was growing increasingly sympathetic to the Irish economic plight. Yet living in, and probably contributing to, the emerging beauty of Dublin's new buildings, Sir William must have been influenced by the Irish Reform movement based there. For, at a time when Parliament's corrupt use of patronage and prejudice had been so effectively exposed by John Wilkes, Sir William's determination to get a British seat seems based on a desire to introduce the new principles of civil liberty to the House. He first stood for election at Canterbury in 1761, but failed at each successive attempt to get the necessary majority. Paradoxically he was finally successful at Canterbury the very year that he concluded the negotiations for the purchase of Gatton. A younger brother, Robert, was thus given the Gatton membership for the time being.

Sir William's maiden speech, in December 1774, was on the rebellious events in America, in which he "condemned the very extraordinary conduct of those in power in withholding from the House the necessary information". It was the Irish who had being crying repeatedly "no taxation without representation" for thirty years before the Americans took up the cry, and Sir William's next speech three days later "drew a melancholy picture of the sufferings of the Irish; said that all promises had been shamefully broken . . . and that the Castle was an asylum to every needy, servile, cringing apostate that would bend the knee and barter everything which should be dear to him, for emolument or court favour." He should know, for his loyalty to Lord North's incompetent administration was soon bought with an Irish peerage, Lord Newhaven of Carrickmayne, and the Mayne partnership was one of those appointed government contractors for victualling troops in North America and the West Indies. Lord Newhaven, as he now was, whilst consistently advocating trade concessions to Ireland and occasionally critical of the North administration's conduct of the war, nevertheless voted with it to the end. In the 1780 election he shared the Gatton seat with his brother, more, one suspects, for fear of otherwise not being returned by the Canterbury electorate, than to get his money's worth. Two years later the family business went bankrupt. William's brother, Robert, committed suicide rather than face the anger of their creditors, which included the Bishop of Salisbury. Partly due to this, and partly due to exasperation at an unresponsive House, — for he opposed the peace preliminaries, objecting to the grant of American independence without adequate provision for the Loyalists — Lord Newhaven lost interest in public affairs and sought to divest himself of his Gatton investment. In October 1783 his nephew wrote: "The Gatton estate is not yet sold, or ever will be at the price his Lordship puts on it — £36,000. This vanity will ruin his Lordship". The fall in value of the rotten borough, by some fifty per cent, is a clear reflection of the anticipated effect of the much expected Parliamentary Reform. Interestingly Sir Robert Clayton, whose family had been the sole patrons of nearby Bletchingley's rotten borough for generations, thought himself lucky to have sold only a few years earlier the reversion in his property to his cousin for only £10,000 on the same grounds.

When Reverend John Tattershall died in 1784, his

trustees delayed selling the estates, waiting on the outcome of Pitt's Reform Bill which included provision to recompense rotten borough patrons to the tune of a million pounds for their loss (supported not surprisingly by Lord Newhaven). But the measure was defeated, and the value of such estates improved with the new future for rotten boroughs. Lord Newhaven then successfully bid for the Upper Gatton portion, thus uniting the Gattons for the first time since the Copley's, and in 1786 conveyed the product to his relatives, the Grahams of Kinross to dispose of as they saw fit. A purchaser for the rest of the Tattershall estate was immediately forthcoming, possibly due to likely candidates being otherwise concerned with the sudden madness of King George III and the likelihood, in the event of the Prince being appointed Regent, of a change of government. The Chipstead tenant with the largest holding, John Fanshawe of Shabden, held Court office and could afford to renew his interest only with the recovery of the King early in 1788. He was still outbid, however, by a member of Parliament who was attached to neither Pitt's nor Fox's parties: William Jolliffe, MP for Petersfield. He was one of only seventeen remaining supporters of Lord North and it was this unlikely member of the *ancien regime* rather than yet another representative of the *nouveau riche* who acquired the majority of the estates, including Merstham and Chipstead. For the first time in generations Merstham was to enjoy a continuous spell of owner occupation, with attendant rector, staff, stables and kennels.

7

RAIL AND ROAD
1786-1807

William Jolliffe's father, the late John Jolliffe, had both City connections and a controlling interest in the Hampshire borough of Petersfield, with its two Parliamentary seats, in the same way that Colebrooke the City banker had lived in, and sat for, Gatton. Following a family tradition, John had ensured his two sons married to advantage. William had married Eleanor the granddaughter of the senior co-heir to the ancient barony of Hylton (then in abeyance), whose family's Durham estates were enriched by the Industrial Revolution's demand for coal. Thomas had married the heiress of Reverend Robert Twyford. William, the elder of the two by a year, had represented Petersfield since 1768 and been rewarded for his loyal support of Lord North with an appointment to the Board of Trade & Plantations in 1772. Holding this post for the next seven years, he was thus involved in the crucial events that finally led to American independence. William Jolliffe's interests in colonial affairs was, however, peripheral to his involvement in the rapid growth of industry in the North. It is significant to Merstham's history that, when Jolliffe opened a new colliery in the north east in 1779, it was linked to the navigable River Wear by a then typical, wooden-railed, waggonway. The family were thus already familiar with this sort of private horse-drawn "railway" that was the forerunner of the first public railways.

The Jolliffe brothers then followed Lord North into brief opposition before North's short-lived coalition with Fox in April 1783. As a member of the coalition government William became a Lord of the Admiralty until driven out of office with the rest of the government on Fox's India Bill that December. Young William (he was thirty-eight at the time) was not left unmoved by the vagaries of politics. Apparently he quarrelled with his neighbours, his relatives and his superiors in the militia, establishing a reputation, in the eyes of a political biographer, of being "whimsical and cantankerous". Certainly his political record is one of objections and opposition to most of the legislation that came before the House during his time there. Further, Gibbon (whose animosity towards Jolliffe dates from their family rivalry over Petersfield) remarked on Jolliffe's "extravagant behaviour, which was much worse than anything you saw in the papers". An ambition of his at this time was to determine the Hylton barony in favour of his wife, briefing Counsel (later Lord Loughborough), urging the claim with successive Prime Ministers, Lord North and the Duke of Portland, and finally having an audience with George III. Having recognised failure at this level, Jolliffe could ignore the subsequent bribe of this peerage from Pitt's chief whip for his support, though it is suprising that he was to remain one of the few not so honoured by the new, young, Prime Minister to facilitate the passage of his economic measures. That year, 1784, his future neighbour, Charles Cocks of Reigate, succeeded in his claim to the Somers peerage, being similarly grandson to the co-heir.

Coincidentally both Jolliffe brothers moved to establish their own country seats at the same time. Thomas moved to Ammerdown, Somerset, following the death of his mother-in-law, and gave up politics, leaving his Petersfield seat for his brother's allies. William left Petersfield after falling out with its burgesses: "They asked more than I could grant; alleging that my house was undertaxed, I made bread at home, bought groceries in London, in short was not so devoted as they expected. Every trifling object of mine was opposed. I was not suffered to plant some trees in the churchyard, and I was opposed in building a wall near my own garden". Jolliffe bought the bulk of the Tattershall estate for

£40,000, but soon found Chipstead society, especially the outbid Fanshawes, no easier to get on with: "every possible report injurious to his character was spread with industry". Accordingly he set about building a house, "The Great House", on the Western outskirts of Merstham village rather than higher up on the Downs. The house was thus set on the northern exposure of the same Greensands that his father's fine house rested on to the south west. Once established at Merstham, Jolliffe pulled down the Petersfield house, though retaining control of its Parliamentary seats. Bearing in mind that the high road through Merstham ran from Marling Glen to the High Street then, access to the Great House was from North Lodge in Gatton Bottom, and from South Lodge in the High Street, now Priors Mead at the end of Quality Street.

The Gatton estate was meanwhile still on the market. Jolliffe was obviously interested, as it would have permitted him to sever all ties with Petersfield while providing him with some control of his neighbours not a mile along the Gatton ridge on which his new house was established. When Samuel Whitbread expressed interest in the borough in 1788, the asking price was £86,000 and, one assumes, such a price was beyond Jolliffe. The following year Newhaven's relatives contracted to sell Gatton for £80,000 to John, Earl of Caithness. With an income of only £700 per annum, the earl suddenly realised the folly of his deal and promptly committed suicide! Eventually that year two London bankers bought the estate: Robert Ladbroke bought Gatton proper for £74,000 and Mark Currie of East Horsley bought Upper Gatton, taking one of the Parliamentary seats in the 1790 election.

Jolliffe concentrated on improving his new estate and radically revised the Merstham and Chipstead tenancies. His choice of Chipstead parish officials was resented by locals who had become used to running their own affairs. Fanshawe succeeded in having Jolliffe convicted for circulating papers to prejudice a jury over the return of parish Overseers of the Poor, which resulted in a six-month prison sentence and £100 fine in November 1791. The stigma of this conviction cost him any remaining chance of resurrecting the Hylton barony claim. When being discussed as much as three years later, it caused an outburst from Lady Spencer "Oh that's monstrous! Just come from the King's bench!". He was not one to trim his sails according to the prevailing wind: When Merstham's rector, Martin Benson, appointed the new Clerk of the parish in 1795, Jolliffe disputed it, again without success. Jolliffe was a good example of one of the industrial capitalists much maligned by an envious squirearchy. When he addressed the poor condition of the existing Croydon-Reigate route through Merstham, William Elliot wrote from Reigate "I seldom trouble myself with country business here, but Jolliffe, who has been driven from his house at Petersfield by his neighbours, has lately bought an estate and is already beginning such a gross job with respect to a turnpike, that every commission is bound in honour and justice to oppose him". The reality was that the Reigate/Sutton Trust feared the potential loss of its toll income from a competing turnpike that not only could offer a better gradient, but also threatened, in its early proposed route, to by-pass Reigate altogether. It was effective opposition from this Trust that kept Jolliffe's turnpike off the statute books for another seventeen years.

Coming, as it did on a tide of radical political reform and the growth of new industrial classes, the French Revolution had a profound effect on the development of English political methods. Alarmed by the anarchy unleashed in the name of Liberty, political factions united in restricting political activity to parliamentary agitation. Alternative clubs or assemblies were legally discouraged. Equally the dislocation to British trade brought about by France's revolutionary wars distracted society's interests to more material matters. For example wheat rose from 43 shillings a quarter in 1792 to 126 shillings in 20 years, the sort of inflation currently taken for granted, but then the most divisive element between town and country. Even from a military perspective the war went badly. By 1797 Britain had no allies, or markets, left on the continent, had lost 40,000 troops in disastrous West Indies campaigns, faced rebellion in Ireland and fleet mutinies at Spithead and the Nore. In the City the financial strain of the war was telling. Even the Bank of England suspended cash payments. Not

Map of Reygate Hundred, 1799

97

surprisingly the London bankers that owned Gatton had had to realise their investment to meet their other commitments. Early in 1796, John Petrie, a recently returned East India merchant, or *nabob*, bought both Gatton estates for £110,000, reserving £50,000 against Colebrooke's debts to the government. He would appear to be the same John Petrie cashiered by Clive for mutiny in 1766 and thereafter active in gun running, decidedly not a worthy successor to the Colebrookes.

In Merstham rent and tithe rose with the price of corn, forcing greater efficiency in food production. Jolliffe consolidated the various smallholdings as they fell in and finally eradicated the medieval strip farming that had survived until then on Ashtead Hill. About this time John Lefevre, whose sister Madelaine was mother of Mark Currie of Upper Gatton, bought Alderstead manor. Gideon Elliot with his large family was the tenant there so the Lefevres were not resident in the parish. Generally Jolliffe was unsympathetic to the French emigrés and found their conduct akin to the "bawling language of a petulant fishwoman". Of Jolliffe's six children, Captain Hylton, the heir, briefly joined his father as a member for Petersfield before rejoining his Coldstream Guards battalion to suppress the Irish revolutionary forces. William had become a curate. Mary had eloped with Captain Hugh Trevor of the 77th Foot, and George, a naval lieutenant, was killed in the heroic battle of the Nile on the *Bellerophon*, the ship with the heaviest British casualties, one third of its entire complement. This decisive victory marked the turning point in Britain's fortunes and Merstham is honoured to have an attractive memorial in St Katharine's commemorating Jolliffe's sacrifice, probably crafted by a local quarryman.

At the turn of the century, when Napoleon had appointed himself the French Republic's First Consul and went on to defeat the armies of the Second Coalition, Pitt resorted to his most daring innovation yet, a tax on incomes. Coincidentally nabob Petrie lost his fortune at the same time and accordingly put his Gatton estate up for auction. In the prevailing economic climate there were, however, few takers. One James Du Pre replaced Petrie, presumably for a price, as Gatton's parliamentary member, but did not purchase the estate. It would seem Du Pre preferred Petersfield with its borough for William Jolliffe certainly contemplated selling it to him at this time. Jolliffe was clearly feeling the pinch, reporting for example that he had "lost £1,500 per annum on his Home Farm for the last three years". Yet, for all the malicious reports of Jolliffe that survive, and the conviction for unduly influencing the choice of parish officials, one testimonial stands out. The then rector, Martin Benson, was quoted as saying "I am happy in being able from my own observation, to bear testimony to the benevolence and liberality of the parish officers. I have known these of many parishes, but I never witnessed any who were so attentive, liberal and humane towards their poor, as those of the parish of Merstham. As an instance it is worthy of observation that, during the whole of that dreadful season 1800-1, when magistrates were overwhelmed with the numerous applications of paupers for relief, no single instance occurred of such an application from this Parish. Their wants here were anticipated and benevolently relieved, at the sole and unbiased instance of the Officers themselves."[11] As advised by his surveyor, Jolliffe had reduced the tenants' rentals (thereby getting relief for the diminished value of his estate) in exchange for taking over the poor rates himself, so that it would be due to him that sufficient funds were made available to the needy of the parish. The first official census, that of 1801, indicates that Merstham was then a relatively small village of 481, compared to Bletchingley's 1,344 (including some 90 "borough" voters), Reigate's 2,246 (of which some 200 could vote) and Croydon's 5,743. Gatton was a hamlet of forty souls, of whom only seven could vote for its two members of Parliament, thus making it the most rotten of all rotten boroughs.

With Napoleon master of Europe, and Nelson master of the surrounding seas, peace was concluded on 1st October 1801. Colonel Hylton Jolliffe had been continuously abroad, under the command of Sir Ralph Abercromby both in the Dutch expedition to Helder Point and then in chasing the French out of Egypt. He did not return to Merstham until the end of that year. Only two months after the return of his eldest son and heir, William Jolliffe became "the victim

99

of a casualty, awful as unforseen" on 18th February 1802. Returning from hunting that day, he stepped backwards through the open trap door of his wine cellar and broke his neck, dying two days later. He remained difficult beyond the grave, as his will caused some argument. But Merstham's tenants were content enough with the new young landlord. Colonel Jolliffe was just twenty-nine when he succeeded to the estate, and the Petersfield parliamentary seat. He took up residence at The Great House giving his brother, William, two acres alongside the Rectory orchard the other side of the main road from him. He built The Cottage, the core of which later became Merstham House.

The taverns of Reigate and Merstham, including The Feathers which must date from this period, had already benefited from the increase in through traffic generated by London Society's new interest in Brighton, made fashionable by the Prince of Wales with his Kremlin-styled Pavilion. They now picked up the extra carriage trade of those Englishmen taking advantage of the peace to swarm across the Channel to sightsee and re-establish trading connections. The treaty of Amiens also restored interest in the hitherto forlorn borough of Gatton. Colonel Mark Wood of the Hon. East India Company, who had returned to England (with a £200,000 fortune in 1793, made whilst chief engineer of Bengal) had spent the war years in Parliament, currying political favour. When he fell out of favour with the influential Duchess of Newcastle, he needed another seat and moved quickly to purchase Gatton for £90,000 out of the proceeds of his Piercefield estate. Once more Gatton was owned by a nabob. Colonel Wood initially shared the Parliamentary membership with his brother-in-law, James Dashwood, but was prevailed upon by the government the following year, 1803, to replace him with Philip Dundas, nephew to Pitt's colleague and former Secretary for War, Lord Melville. It is in keeping with Gatton's dubious reputation that, when the government wished to replace Dundas with another appointee in 1805, the opposition counterbid £10,000 for their own candidate. The Gatton residents were not, apparently, as corrupt as their political masters: According to Farringdon "the voters are limited to the parish of Gatton, and there are only seven tenants in

Former House of Commons 1808
(Courtesy of The Guildhall Library, Corporation of London)

the parish, and to them only is the privilege of voting confined. Wood does not let what is tenanted at, on an average, more than 30 shillings an acre. It is remarkable that the tenants have been incorruptible to bribery, though attempted with large offers, such as £500 each. The same families have for a considerable time continued upon the farms, from father to son. They all hold the estates from year to year". In fact Colonel Wood was the only resident to hold his house freehold, the remaining six houses being let by him by the week.

In October 1802 Hylton and William Jolliffe attended the Reigate Petty Sessions to hear the proposal from a sub-committee of the newly created Surrey Iron Railway Company for an extension of its Wandsworth to Croydon railway, then still under construction, to Merstham and beyond. This "vast and important concern", The Surrey Iron Railway, had been sanctioned by Parliamentary Act the previous year as the first public railway, and had been set up by a group of Wandle valley industrialists in direct competition to a proposed Croydon Canal, also sanctioned by an Act of the same year, to provide the first stage of improved communications to Portsmouth's vital dockyards. William Jessop already known for his flanged tramlines, or "edge rails", the surveyor for the project, had convinced the promoters that a plate railway for horse-drawn waggons was a viable alternative to a canal in linking the City to its nearest corn market to the south, Croydon. The extension from there southwards would naturally follow the easiest gradients through the Downs to Merstham, branching south east to the coast via Godstone, and south west to Portsmouth via Reigate as appropriate. There were doubts expressed on the ability to pass through Reigate where the extension would be "shut up by Mr Mowbray's Park", but the Jolliffe brothers were supportive of its passing through their estate, to the delight of Jessop. "It is extremely fortunate that it is directed through the very valuable quarries of Lime Stone at Merstham, apparently superior in quality for Water Proof Lime to either that of Guildford or Dorking. The probable consumption of which in London will be very great; for it may be sold there as cheap as the common Chalk-Lime, as one horse will draw 10 tons of it to Wandsworth in four hours". In fact the Jolliffe brothers' support of the project was to have a significant impact not only on the fortunes of their family, but also on the future of Merstham.

The renewal of war against Napoleon in May 1803, and the threat of his imminent invasion of England, spurred the Croydon, Merstham & Godstone Iron Railway Act onto the statute books only two months ahead of the Surrey Iron Railway being officially opened to Croydon. The rival canal scheme, meanwhile, had barely made any progress. John Rennie, already well known for several civil engineering projects, had been brought in to formulate the Croydon to Portsmouth canal proposals. The resulting Parliamentary bill was frustrated in March 1804, largely through the efforts of the member for Petersfield, Colonel Jolliffe. The war with France being entirely naval at this stage, Hylton was able to resign his commission and concentrate on his political and domestic concerns (while naval Captain James

Wood, Mark's younger brother, gave up his Gatton seat for active service in the Caribbean). The neighbouring MPs were both retired military gentlemen and Tory, but of different persuasions. Colonel Wood, a Scotsman with an HEIC commission and twenty-three years older than Jolliffe, supported the ministers of Pitt's new government. Colonel Jolliffe, a retired King's officer, was a friend and contemporary of George Canning, Pitt's young disciple, making him a more independent Tory, like his father before him. That September he married nineteen-year-old Rose Elizabeth Shirley, the natural daughter of the Earl of Ferrers, and brought her back to her new home at The Great House, just as the first railway "navvies" reached Merstham village.

The Grand Surrey Railway, as the joint SIR and CMG lines were referred to, followed the main road down Hooley valley to Harps Oak Lane, where it curved away to the east to service the quarries beneath modern Shepherds Hill. Nothing more ambitious than canal-style cuttings up to twenty-six feet deep were attempted to ease the gradient of the Downs, but even this was no easy task in those non-mechanical days. Merstham's parish register records the accidental death of a railway labourer in a winter land-slip. Nevertheless the line was opened with great publicity on 24th July 1805. Such periodicals as *Sporting Anecdotes* and the *Annual Register* recorded how one Mr Banks won a wager by demonstrating how a single horse could pull over fifty tons along six miles of the railway at an average speed of almost four mph, a significant contender to the typical canal loads of the time. Although the first steam locomotives were already in existence, it was twenty-five years before they became a serious alternative to the horse. As one authority of the time said "Does anyone in possession of his senses expect that this snorting, spluttering, hideous machine of iron, beltching forth smoke and steam, can ever accomplish such a draught as is easily undertaken by the horses of the Surrey Iron Road?". Traces of the Merstham cutting are still visible beside London Road North, while Weighbridge Cottage was constructed at about this time purely for the purpose that its name suggests: the determination of the toll payable by the wagon owners. A section of the railway is now displayed opposite The Feathers. The line was never extended further south once Nelson's destruction of the combined enemy fleets off Trafalgar removed the sense of urgency that had dominated the initial undertaking.

It is now that the shape of Merstham changed to resemble its more modern configuration. The Jolliffes took this opportunity to develop the labourers' route that followed the railway line, and build a new road to the East of St Katharine's, rejoining the High Street at The Feathers, which effectively by-passed both the steeper gradient of the old road over Merstham Hill (modern Church Hill) and the brothers' estates between Gatton Bottom and The Feathers. For this purpose an Act of Parliament was obtained in 1807 (Jolliffe's friend, George Canning had been returned to high office in the new Portland ministry) and the Jolliffes' long-awaited turnpike was finally established, from Croydon via Merstham on what is now the A23 as far as Gatton Point, "then over Ray common, into Reigate. With such spirit was the work carried on, that the whole was very speedily completed". The improved communications put the locality more in touch with national events. Inevitably it was news of turf and ring events that was of greater interest than despatches from the Peninsular campaign, but Merstham was soon sharply reminded of the war when the wounded from the disastrous Walcheren expedition of 1809 were quartered in the locality.

The contractor for constructing this new turnpike was a partnership formed for the occasion, between the Jolliffe brothers and one Edward Banks. The latter was not necessarily the same Mr Banks that had wagered so successfully over the pulling power of the Iron Railway, but it may explain the often-quoted myth that Edward Banks started his impressive career on the Surrey Iron Railway. Certainly, as his Chipstead monument states, his origins were humble; he was a Yorkshire-bred navvy who had followed in Jessop's footsteps. But while the CMG line was being built in Surrey, Edward Banks was the contractor responsible for building a new turnpike in Derbyshire. He may well have been introduced to the Jolliffes by any one of the CMG connections: Jessop, Outram or the Butterley Company engineers, all of whom had been previous employers of Banks' expertise. As explained later Hylton's interest in the partnership was soon eclipsed by that of his brother, William. On the face of it, it is difficult to imagine a stranger partnership than that of the clerical younger son of the landed gentry and the cabin boy turned drainage engineer with a host of successful contracts already to his credit. Yet, perhaps because William at thirty-three was close enough to his own north country origins, the two got on well enough together for their partnership to last the next twenty-seven busy years. Indeed, with Jolliffe's finance and Banks' engineering skill together with both their networks of useful connections, it is not surprising to find the Jolliffe & Banks partnership soon became the most important firm of civil engineering contractors of its time.

8

BUILDINGS AND BARONETS
1808-1836

Apart from taking a substantial amount of traffic from the longer Sutton/Reigate turnpike, the new road also brought trade to the Merstham railhead. Fuller's earth for use in the Yorkshire cloth industry, was one local freight, from Nutfield, that was "carried in waggons, each drawing from three to four tons, to the beginning of the iron railway, near Merstham, along which it is taken to the banks of the Thames, where it is sold at the different wharfs". Equally, and as predicted by Jessop, "great quantities of chalk [from Jolliffes' quarries] have been conveyed by this means to the vicinity of the metropolis, and the business of lime burning is carried on with great alacrity". The Jolliffes developed their chalk and lime works out of Merstham's medieval stone quarries to great effect. While the Grand Surrey Railway did little financially for its shareholders, especially once the Croydon canal opened in 1809 to the detriment of the SIR section, there can be no doubt that it brought some gain to its Merstham and Nutfield users. It also provided a record level of employment to the village; in the first decade of the century its population grew by thirty-eight per cent, the next decade by a further twenty per cent. Arthur Bryant called this latter period the "Age of Elegance"; with the dust of the up-traffic and the strench of the manure brought down from town, the very opposite must have been Merstham's lot. Improvements in communication have

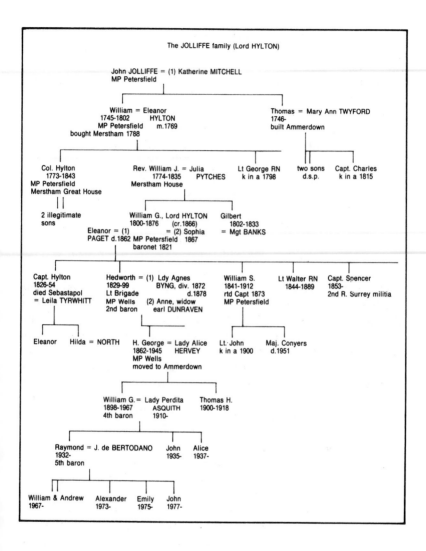

The JOLLIFFE family (Lord HYLTON)

John JOLLIFFE = (1) Katherine MITCHELL
MP Petersfield

William = Eleanor
1745-1802 HYLTON
MP Petersfield m.1769
bought Merstham 1788

Thomas = Mary Ann TWYFORD
1746-
built Ammerdown

Col. Hylton
1773-1843
MP Petersfield
Merstham Great House

Rev. William J. = Julia
1774-1835 PYTCHES
Merstham House

Lt George RN
k in a 1798

two sons
d.s.p.

Capt. Charles
k in a 1815

2 illegitimate
sons

William G., Lord HYLTON
1800-1876 (cr.1866)
Eleanor = (1) = (2) Sophia
PAGET d.1862 MP Petersfield 1867
baronet 1821

Gilbert
1802-1833
= Mgt BANKS

Capt. Hylton
1826-54
died Sebastapol
= Leila TYRWHITT

Hedworth = (1) Ldy Agnes
1829-99 BYNG, div. 1872
Lt Brigade d.1878
MP Wells (2) Anne, widow
2nd baron earl DUNRAVEN

William S.
1841-1912
rtd Capt 1873
MP Petersfield

Lt Walter RN
1844-1889

Capt. Spencer
1853-
2nd R. Surrey militia

Eleanor

Hilda = NORTH

H. George = Lady Alice
1862-1945 HERVEY
MP Wells
moved to Ammerdown

Lt. John
k in a 1900

Maj. Conyers
d.1951

William G. = Lady Perdita
1898-1967 ASQUITH
4th baron 1910-

Thomas H.
1900-1918

Raymond = J. de BERTODANO
1932-
5th baron

John
1935-

Alice
1937-

William & Andrew
1967-

Alexander
1973-

Emily
1975-

John
1977-

always been a mixed blessing, and since then Merstham has always been one of the first to "enjoy" the latest traffic methods.

One of those who benefited from the Jolliffes' enterprise was one George Hall, the founder of the builders' merchants, Hall & Co. Ltd., well known locally until it was absorbed into the RMC group in the 1960s. George Hall was one of those wretched youths wandering in search of employment in the 1800/1 depression, who had been helped by the generosity of the Jolliffes. Given work in the Merstham quarries, he had soon risen to a position of some responsibility, though it was to be some years yet before he took over the quarry lease from Jolliffe & Banks. The extent to which both Jolliffes were largely "sleeping partners" in the quarries can be surmised from their share of profits: The 1813 profit of £8,500 was shared 3% to Hylton Jolliffe, 12% to William Jolliffe and 85% to Edward Banks. In taking the workings deeper into the Downs, the firm had to construct a half-mile drainage adit. This caused such a drop in the local water table, that the lessee of Merstham's mill (a water mill had been operated south east of St Katharine's since at least Norman times), Thomas Durrant, sued successfully for loss of earnings and received £2,000 in compensation. As he had built a windmill on Rockshaw ridge some years previously, Durrant was still able to act as the village miller in the eleven year interval that his water mill stood idle.

Colonel Jolliffe's interest in Merstham waned somewhat following the death of his childless young wife in 1809. As long as he remained a widower, and despite having a couple of illegitimate sons, Colonel Jolliffe could now expect his estates to pass eventually through his brother William, whose earlier marriage to Julia Pitches had already been blessed with two sons, William and Gilbert. Accordingly Hylton moved to London, leaving the routine estate duties to his brother. He continued to visit Merstham, especially for the hunting that he and his brother had developed. While still very much a "Canningite" (and Canning was now much out of favour following his quarrel and duel with Castlereagh), Hylton never took his position too seriously, in contrast to his country neighbour, Mark Wood.

Mark Wood had applied for various senior overseas

positions, but was considered by the government as "quite overrun with folly and self conceit". Being ambitious for his sons, he also applied for a baronetcy, which he finally received in 1808, though without any accompanying post. As Sir George Colebrooke retained the "Gatton" baronetcy title, he became Sir Mark Wood of "Gatton Park" in Upper Gatton. The following year his batchelor brother, Commodore James Wood, who had distinguished himself in the capture of Curacao in 1807, received a knighthood. This probably explains why Sir Mark Wood was prepared to vote with the ministers to bestow the regency on the Prince of Wales (who was expected to introduce his Whig friends to government), while Jolliffe voted against. In the election of 1812 that followed the assassination of Perceval, the new Prime Minister, Sir Mark Wood, ever in search of further favour, shared his borough with William Congreve, a close friend of the Prince Regent but better known to history for his military rockets. Colonel Jolliffe at the same time offered to share his Petersfield borough with George Canning as insurance against his possible defeat at Liverpool. In the event Canning achieved a personal triumph in being returned by a trading electorate much impressed by his opposition to an earlier American intercourse bill. Wood further supported the Regent in duly opposing Catholic Relief, while Jolliffe sided with those who felt commissions should not be restricted to the pre-Union Irish officers, and voted repeatedly for the unsuccessful bills.

Rather than continue to leave The Great House empty, Hylton let it in 1813 to one John Dean Paul and his family. John Paul was qualified in civil law, two years younger than Hylton, and ran a successful banking and naval agency business from London's West End. The Great House was occupied by his wife, seven children and his mother-in-law, Lady Ann Simpson. William Jolliffe's wife noted in her diary: "Our families at the Great House and The Cottage quickly became on intimate terms and remained great friends to the end".[15] At the same time Wood let Upper Gatton House to William Beauclerk, brother of the sixth Duke of St. Albans, with his family of ten children.

Peace came to a shattered Europe the following year and Merstham's noteworthy travellers were not so much the wealthy southward-bound sightseers as the destitute north-ward-bound released prisoners of war. Then came Napoleon's brief return culminating in the Battle of Waterloo. One of those who fell in this final victory was a cousin of Hylton, Captain Charles Jolliffe who was Thomas Jolliffe of Ammerdown's youngest son. He had served at Copenhagen, in North America, the West Indies and Spain, being severely wounded at Ortes. "He had not entirely recovered from this wound when the toscin of war once more summoned him to the field of battle". Thus both branches of the Jolliffe family had lost youngest sons in decisive victories. Perhaps the Merstham Jolliffes visited Ammerdown in the wake of this loss, for they were away from Surrey for the critical post-war depression. The immediate drop in food prices, enforced by a drastic Corn Law, caused acute agricultural distress, frequently intensified by the unwise administration of the Poor Laws, which in certain parts of the country led to alarming political agitation. That Surrey should be one of the worst offenders may well have something to do with William Cobbett, the Radical Reformer recently fled to America, being a native of West Surrey. Certainly "riots and outrages, such as we associate with the worst districts of Ireland in bad times, were common within thirty miles of London". Respect for the Jolliffe administration (and alternative employment in the quarries or in service with the newly-titled local households) kept Merstham peaceful throughout these troubled times, and it must have been with a sense of relief that the family were welcomed home. On their return Mrs Jolliffe recorded, not only did they ring St Katharine's bells but the following day "the bells continued ringing all morning. Miss Paul came over to see us, and Mr Jolliffe arrived from Town. Mr William and Mr Jolliffe went out hunting. We dined at Mr Paul's. The duke and duchess of St Albans were there". For William Beauclerk had only months earlier become the eighth duke following the sudden death of his infant nephew and sister-in-law.

On the positive side the war years had given great impetus to several engineering projects that might otherwise have foundered on lack of perceived benefit in relation to cost. The list of such enterprises for which the Jolliffe &

Banks partnership was responsible is impressive: Dartmoor prison and Dublin's Howth Harbour in 1810, dockyard work along the Thames at West India Docks in 1811, Sheerness Dockyards from 1813 to 1830, Deptford and London Docks in 1817, Waterloo and Southwark bridges from 1812 and 1816 respectively. For all but the Dartmoor prison project the partnership worked to John Rennie's designs so that their difference of opinion over the Portsmouth canal was long since forgotten. Closer to home, the London to Brighton road brought increasing traffic through Merstham: From 1810 the Royal Night Mail coaches became regular users and after 1816, when the new Gatton Point to Horley toll road cut the distance still further, public coaches were running between London and Brighton on the modern A23 route at the rate of fifty-two a day. Some would have stopped at Jolliffe's inns: The Star at Hooley, the Fox Inn (now Fox Shaw) north of Harps Oak, the Hylton Arms (later Jolliffe Arms and now Detroits) at the bottom of Shepherds Hill, or The Feathers at Merstham. William Jolliffe could now afford to make the first additions to The Cottages in 1817, employing Lord Derby's gardener to plant new trees from France in the grounds. The following year Mrs Jolliffe noted: "Waterloo bridge was opened with great ceremony on 18th June [the battle's anniversary], Messrs Jolliffe & Banks, the contractors, receiving no small praise". The total cost, including land, of Waterloo Bridge was over a million pounds. It has since been replaced but at the time it represented the first London use of Aberdeenshire granite.

Possibly in this connection and possibly since Canning had been reconciled to the government with the cabinet post of president of the Board of Control, Hylton renewed the family's claim to the Hylton barony with the Prime Minister, Lord Liverpool, that year. He was offered instead a baronetcy which he declined for himself but accepted for his nephew, young William, on his majority. Apart from being known for his sporting interests, and taste in hats, "Colonel Jolliffe", as a writer in the *Sporting Magazine* said, "is liberal to all his dependants, hospitable to his neighbours, evenhanded to all. Full of cheerfulness and charity, his inward qualities command my esteem. No one can be kinder or more polite to friend or stranger. Beloved by all his tenants, the very idol of his tenantry. He settles all claims of damage himself on the spot when hunting, paying ample compensation". Hunting events were taken seriously: Finding the Master of the Old Surrey Foxhounds had dug out a fox on his Merstham hunting grounds in 1818, he determined to settle the matter with a duel on Alderstead Heath. Both parties fired wide and repaired to The Great House for breakfast together!

As part of his education, Hylton's nephew had become a lieutenant in the yeomanry. It was in this capacity the following year that the nineteen-year-old heir came face to face with the rebellious discontent of the provinces. For young Lieutenant Jolliffe was with those attempting to arrest a popular agitator, Henry Hunt, in Manchester when they had to be rescued from the mob by the 15th Hussars in what was later called the "Peterloo massacre". Later he recalled how shocked he was at how so many had been caught in the crush of the moment and how the injured included women and children. It was a dramatic introduction to politics for a member of a family hitherto associated with the liberal Toryism of Canning. Following George IV's coronation in 1821, through the prior agreement between his uncle and Lord Liverpool, Lieutenant Jolliffe became Sir William Jolliffe of Merstham while still only twenty. Only days later John Paul became Sir John Paul of Rodburgh, resurrecting an earlier family baronetcy. The Pauls had left Merstham following the death of Lady Ann Simpson on 26th March 1821. A memorial to her, as daughter of the 8th Earl of Strathmore, was placed in St Katharine's by Mrs Paul. Thus ended Merstham's brief connection with this ancestor of Queen Elizabeth, the Queen Mother. (It might also be mentioned, though, that Sir John Paul's same named son married Georgiana Beauclerk, a cousin of the Upper Gatton residents, and set up house in South Nutfield. He achieved notoriety some thirty years later when prosecuted in 1855 for his share in his banking firm's massive fraud). This allowed Colonel Hylton Jolliffe to move back into The Great House where he acted as host to his nephew's coming of age. Despite the winter conditions: "Church bells rang all day. Flags were hung out on the

Peterloo, Manchester, 26th August 1819. The future
Lord Hylton's introduction to politics.

house and church. Every poor family in Merstham had
meat, bread and a bushel of coals. Presents were given to all
the servants. The whole village were invited to a dance in
the Great Hall and three hundred people attended", noted
his mother that December.

By then the Jolliffe & Banks partnership had lost their
favourite patron. For sixty-year-old John Rennie died that
October, leaving among other things, his design for

replacing the famous medieval London Bridge, incorporating the by then familiar Rennie flat roadway. His two sons, George and John Rennie, continued the work of his projects with Messrs Jolliffe and Banks, some twenty years their senior. Not long after the late John Rennie was buried in St Paul's cathedral, Edward Banks received a knighthood, the first such awarded to a civil engineer. Reverend William Jolliffe may well have had a hand in the matter (Canning had succeeded Castlereagh at the Foreign Office) to assist Banks' marriage. Bearing in mind that twenty-five years earlier Jolliffe himself had had to overcome tremendous family opposition to his own courting of one of the Pitches girls, he would have enjoyed making certain that his sister-in-law Amelia Pitches, married no less than someone with a knighthood! It was Sir Edward Banks' second marriage, his previous wife having died some years earlier. That year the City's New Bridge Committee chose Rennie's design and the necessary Act received Royal Assent in 1823. Jolliffe and Banks were awarded the six-year contract at £506,000. The partners then set up a new venture, The General Steam Navigation Company capitalised at £200,000, which would include responsibility for shipping granite from Aberdeen and Dartmoor for the new bridge. The first stone was laid with great ceremony in 1825. The prosperous partnership had been further cemented in 1823 by the marriage of Edward Banks' daughter, Margaret, to Reverend William Jolliffe's other son, Gilbert Jolliffe, who by then was a dashing young cavalry officer with the 19th Light Dragoons. The young couple initially lived with the Banks at Hooley, below Chipstead just north of Merstham. Both young Jolliffes, Sir William and Gilbert, were well positioned in society, their mother noting with pride how they escorted the Duke of Gloucester back from Epsom races to stay at Merstham House, as the enlarged Cottage was now called. Colonel Hylton Jolliffe's Great House had become Merstham Hall. In 1825 it was Sir William's turn to be married. That October he married seventeen-year-old Eleanor Paget at St James' Westminster. Hylton Jolliffe obviously had every confidence in his nephew and very generously made a gift of all his Surrey estates to the newly married couple.

Although Colonel Hylton Jolliffe's main residence was in

London, he still frequented Merstham, carrying out the usual country pursuits of the time in the company of his relatives and friends. The *Gentleman's Magazine* of 1830 introduces Roffey, another family long-connected with Merstham: "The Colonel as a Fox Hunter is known all the world over, but old Roffey, the Huntsman, is the boy for me — stands about six foot and turns the scales at fifteen stone, out of deference to the Colonel's sixteen stone! For thirty years Surrey has had his benefit, but in years both he and the Colonel are outstripped by "Yorkshire Jack" the Whip. He and his wife and Roffey and his wife have snug little hunting boxes facing the road and in front of the kennels. The house and kennels are situated at the entrance of the neat and pretty village of Merstham. The only fault is that the kennels are too near the high road. The arrangements are good and there is running water in the yard." There is an oil painting owned by the Morris family, which depicts the pack in Church meadows below St Katherine's with Roffey and Yorkshire Jack in the Jolliffe livery. The Roffey family lived at Merstham Grange at the south west end of the High Street.

In neighbouring Gatton the elderly Sir Mark Wood had, he felt, had a poor return on his political investment. It is understandable then how his son, also called Mark, took no interest in politics or the Gatton family seat. When his father died in 1829, Mark was thirty-five, unmarried and "well known in sporting circles". Having succeeded to the Gatton baronetcy he immediately looked to sell the estate. It was a critical moment. A poor harvest and a hard winter that year — so hard that Merstham's pack of hounds were put down — kept property values low. Agricultural wages had fallen 10 per cent, from 5/- to 4/6d or less a week, causing enough distress for the militia to be called in to restore order in nearby Dorking. According to Merstham's rector this "most alarming spirit of discontent and insubordination . . . showed itself but little in these parts, in as much as our farmers had been liberal towards their labourers and the poor, and as rent and tithes had been previously reduced". But the death of George IV in June 1830 meant a General Election at a time when the ruling Tories were still reeling from the divisions caused by

Jolliffe & Banks contractors replacing London Bridge
1831. A bit of each bridge is preserved in Merstham.

Catholic Emancipation. A captive borough might yet
attract a premium. In July that year Sir Mark Wood
successfully sold Gatton to the trustees of twenty-one-year-
old Lord Monson, for £100,000. Within days news broke of
the Paris rising and the spectre of Revolution spread across
Europe. The Radicals were delighted; the new parliament
was bound to reconsider Parliamentary Reform. William
Cobbett, who had returned refreshed from the States some
years earlier, published his *Rural Rides* that year, in which
Gatton is described by him as "a very rascally spot of
earth". Gatton at that time had 23 houses and 146 people
of whom only seven could vote. With the advantage of
hindsight it is clear that Monson's trustees had paid a
ridiculous price for a rotten borough of uncertain future.
King William IV asked Grey to form the first Whig
administration since the days of Charles Fox.

It was the same King who officially opened the new
London Bridge on 1st August 1831. The delay experienced
by Jolliffe and Banks was due to the difficulties caused by

keeping the old bridge in use throughout the seven years of construction. The doubly-constricted tides accounted for most of the ten souls lost in the construction work, while the cost overran by thirty-four per cent. (As well as contemporary prints done by Edward Cooke there are some watercolours by Major Yates of the construction. They remain in the Jolliffe family.) John Rennie received a knighthood and his contractors then got on with the job of demolishing the old bridge. Whilst most of its arches had been repaired over time and it had long since lost its housing superstructure, the old bridge's base dated from 1209. One piece of the old bridge, a sculptured stone shield with three leopards on it, was placed by Jolliffe in the tower arch of St Katharine's in Merstham. More recently, a piece of granite from Rennie's London Bridge, unnoticed in the removal of the bridge to the States, was placed in Marling Glen where it has been made into a large milestone.

Frederick John Monson was the fifth Baron Monson, descended from the Royalist cousin of the regicide Monson last associated with the locality in the Civil War. While each eldest son kept the title polished through good marriages, the performance of the junior sons was more lacklustre. One, Colonel George Monson, had devoted most of his time in India to trying to bring down Warren Hastings. Another, his nephew, was unfortunately known only for his "retreat, defeats, disgraces, and disasters" in the Mahratta campaign of 1804. Frederick's father was an eldest son, and had been the fourth Lord Monson only long enough to get married and see the birth of his only son. His widow, Lady Sarah, seven years later married the Earl of Warwick. One searches in vain for a reason why this well-established and well-connected Lincolnshire family should look to purchase an alternative seat at Gatton. In 1831 Monson duly return two members for the borough, his cousin John Saville, eldest son of the Earl of Mexborough, and John Ashley Cooper, fourth son of the Earl of Shaftesbury. They were the last to represent Gatton in Parliament. The frail young lord put up a good fight; he was one of only twenty-two "stalwart" peers to vote against the Reform bill, once the Duke of Wellington had conceded through abstention rather than face the wholesale creation

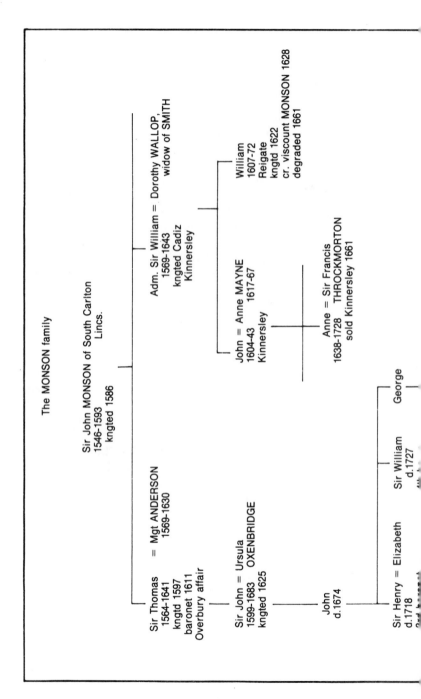

The MONSON family

Sir John MONSON of South Carlton
Lincs.
1546-1593
kngted 1586

Sir Thomas = Mgt ANDERSON
1564-1641   1569-1630
kngtd 1597
baronet 1611
Overbury affair

Adm. Sir William = Dorothy WALLOP,
1569-1643   widow of SMITH
kngted Cadiz
Kinnersley

Sir John = Ursula OXENBRIDGE
1599-1683
kngted 1625

John = Anne MAYNE
1604-43   1617-67
Kinnersley

William
1607-72
Reigate
kngtd 1622
cr. viscount MONSON 1628
degraded 1661

John
d.1674

Anne = Sir Francis
1638-1728   THROCKMORTON
sold Kinnersley 1661

Sir Henry = Elizabeth
d.1718

George

Sir William
d.1727

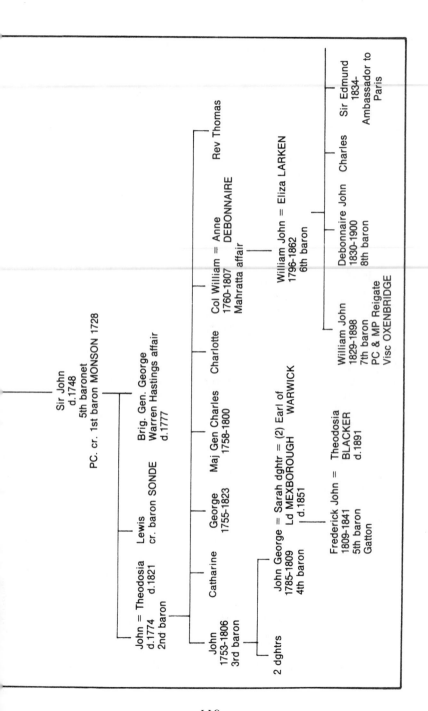

Sir John
d.1748
5th baronet
PC. cr. 1st baron MONSON 1728

John = Theodosia   Lewis   Brig. Gen. George
d.1774   d.1821   cr. baron SONDE   Warren Hastings affair
2nd baron   d.1777

John   Catharine   George   Maj Gen Charles   Charlotte   Col William = Anne   Rev Thomas
1753-1806   1755-1823 1758-1800   1760-1807   DEBONNAIRE
3rd baron   Mahratta affair

2 dghtrs   John George = Sarah dghtr = (2) Earl of   William John = Eliza LARKEN
            1785-1809   Ld MEXBOROUGH   WARWICK   1796-1862
            4th baron   d.1851   6th baron

            Frederick John = Theodosia   William John   Debonnaire John   Charles   Sir Edmund
            1809-1841   BLACKER   1829-1898   1830-1900   1834-
            5th baron   d.1891   7th baron   8th baron   Ambassador to
            Gatton   PC & MP Reigate   Paris
                                              Visc OXENBRIDGE

119

of Whig peers by an unwilling King. The Reform Act of 1832 abolished Gatton's parliamentary status, first established 380 years previously. In Surrey, Bletchingley and Haslemere were the other rotten boroughs abolished, while Reigate lost one of its two seats. A new borough of Lambeth was created, and the county representation was doubled to four members. Only Guildford and Southwark boroughs were left undisturbed.

Hylton Jolliffe had represented Petersfield since 1802. He stepped down briefly in 1830 in favour of his two nephews, Sir William and Gilbert, but took back his seat from Gilbert for the 1831 parliament. After the Reform Act cut this borough down to a single seat with a much enlarged local electorate, Hylton Jolliffe tried for it, only to find it contested by a Whig with Merstham connections. It will be recalled that Merstham's Alderstead manor had been purchased by John Lefevre in the 1790s. His heiress married Charles Shaw who then inherited by becoming Charles Shaw Lefevre. His eldest son, Charles, was married to a sister of Samuel Whitbread and in 1830 began a long and eminent career as a Whig politician. The other son, John, was another Whig, a founder member of the Athenaeum Club and only some three years older than Sir William Jolliffe. The Shaw Lefevres, being now Hampshire-based, had sold Alderstead to Jolliffe before 1831, but the first election after the Reform Act brought them together as opponents in Petersfield. John Shaw Lefevre won the seat in the December 1832 election by one vote, but the ballot must have been questionable, for Hylton Jolliffe was seated by petition the following year.

It was a reminder to Hylton of the widening generation gap. By 1834 both Jolliffe brothers were about sixty and agreed with Sir Edward Banks to retire their partnership. Within a year Reverend William Jolliffe and Sir Edward Banks were dead. Sir Edward Banks had been staying with his widowed daughter, Mrs Jolliffe, at Tilgate, Sussex, at the time of his death, but was buried at St Margaret's, Chipstead, according to his wishes, since first "struck with the beauty of the neighbouring hamlet". Apart from his appropriately ornate tomb, there is also a memorial to his achievements within the church. In 1834 Merstham Hall,

The marble hall, Gatton
Monson's marble hall was modelled on a baroque
chapel in Rome. The frescos, by Joseph Severn,
depicted Esther as Prudence, Ruth as Meekness,
Penelope as Patience and Queen Eleanor as Fortitude.

previously the Great House, was pulled down as unsafe, the
materials and fixtures being sold to Lord Monson along the
ridge for £1,000 and used in his reconstruction of Gatton
Hall. For Frederick Monson had done the Grand Tour of
classical Europe (possibly in the company of his cousin,
William John Monson, who had published a journal of his
tours in "Istria, Dalmatia, Sicily, Malta and Calabria") and
was determined to restyle Gatton in the newly-fashionable
Italian style. The previously plain stone building was

virtually rebuilt in some of the finest Italian marble. St Andrew's church, which had been neglected to the point of being used merely as a barn, was also changed, from a typical English perpendicular into a romantic Gothic style. The furnishings of both the house and church were collected from his tours, at a time when the revolutionary authorities on the Continent "were prepared to sell off ecclesiastical treasures with an eye only to their secular values". Frederick Monson had married Theodosia Blacker in 1832 but the couple were destined never to have children, in contrast to their Jolliffe neighbours who ended up with at least a dozen.

The work at Gatton was bound to take some years. In the meantime the Monsons were frequent visitors to Warwick Castle where Lord Monson's mother held court. The Duchess de Dino described them there in 1834: "The Countess of Warwick is "the least appropriate possible for the position she occupies. She was pretty without being beautiful . . . she has an amusing character and not at all staid, her bearing is relaxed, and this stout little, lazy, idle lady doesn't seem at all suitable to govern this huge, serious and almost formidable abode"; while her son, Lord Monson, is "a little figure of a man, or rather child, timid and quiet, embarrassed at his small height and his weak body. Lady Monson contrasts strongly with her husband, a large fair Englishwoman, rigid, bony with long features, large hands, a large flat chest, a look of a big girl, angular movements, *tout d'une piece*, but polite and attentive".[16] This snapshot may not do them full justice. Apart from his political and artistic dedication, Lord Monson set up the Surrey Lodge of Freemasons (with Gatton's young rector, Reverend J. C. Wynter, as treasurer) in 1834, becoming Provincial Grand Master in 1836. It was also he, rather than Jolliffe, who later determined that the London & Brighton Railway should have a station at Merstham.

The reformed parliament got off to a shaky start: The Whig cabinet was unable to fulfil the Radicals' expectations (those in Merstham's High Street on 4th February 1834 saw the *Criterion* coach take the political news from London to Brighton in a record 3 hours, 40 minutes!), and Hylton Jolliffe's return to Parliament was just in time to witness the rapid turnover of the Grey, Melbourne and Peel administrations in a matter of months. At the next election, in 1835, he was again unable to secure the support of the Petersfield electorate by 87 votes to 103, losing this time to C. J. Hector who had been the Jolliffe family's Petersfield steward for over thirty years, now an ardent radical reformer. It was too much of a humiliation for the Colonel. In the 1837 election he left it to his young nephew to challenge Hector. Sir William won by one vote but was unseated by petition in February 1838. The young baronet's taste for politics remained however. Of the two other baronetcies associated with the area, that of Gatton passed in 1838 to Henry Thomas Colebrooke's son, Thomas, whose own son was to become Lord Colebrooke almost seventy years later, while that of Gatton Park went into temporary abeyance: Sir Mark Wood had reinvested the proceeds of Gatton's sale in Hare Park near Newmarket and finally married in 1833. He was only forty-five when he died four years later, remembered as "much attached to the sport of the turf, of which he was a constant and liberal patron; and has left a large and valuable breeding stud." As he had only daughters, the title died with him, not to be resurrected for another sixty years.

Despite the many political changes of this period, the country villages had changed little for generations. Work for most people was within easy walking distance and few would have travelled much beyond their parish. A tithe map for Merstham at this time gives a clear idea of the parish before the new railways changed the rural way of life. It tells us that commercial Merstham, apart from the quarry, was 66 per cent arable, 25 per cent pasture and 9 per cent woodland, presumably a reverse sequence of the mix in medieval times. The farm with the highest tithe value was that of Alderstead (£512), then tenanted by William Golds. Next was Dean Farm, Hooley (£316), then Wellhead and Home farms (£218 equally). Michael Stacey tenanted Home Farm, virtually all of whose fields stretched along Rockshaw ridge. Robert Roffey tenanted Albury Farm with double the value of neighbouring Battlebridge Farm when John Dives paid rent to Lord Monson. For, apart from the Glebe and common land, the Jolliffes only owned about 83 per cent of Merstham parish. William Bristow owned Oakley farm, letting it to one John Brooker, while the smallholdings of Nokeland and Marsh Farm were owner-occupied by Archibald Little and Robert Clement respectively. George Hall had the lease of the lime works below Shepherds Hill, and it is perhaps appropriate that it was his artistic granddaughter, Jessie Hall, Merstham born and bred, who later evoked the calm pastoral scenes of farming on the Downs (popularised on Edwardian Chistmas cards) before such farming methods disappeared altogether.

9

PEERS' PATRONAGE
1837-1877

The accession of eighteen-year-old Victoria gave a sense of stability to the country after the traumas associated with her elderly uncles. Despite the muddles of Melbourne's Irish, Canadian and Jamaican measures, and despite new levels of widespread distress and government deficits, there was a thrill of purposeful movement: Countrymen moved to the towns; coal was moved to the mills and the docks; steam engines powered the looms, the ships, and especially the railways. The railway was the major factor in the growth and expansion not only of the country generally, but of the localities it served especially. The 1829 Rainhill trails had finally established steam traction as a serious contender to the horses that were still being used extensively on a number of railways, not only the Grand Surrey Railway. This very rapidly led to a rash of new railways: London's first such was to Greenwich in 1833. The London & Croydon Railway Act was passed in 1835 including provision for the purchase of the now moribund Croydon canal, with a view to it linking up with the Greenwich line at its new London Bridge terminus. The South Eastern Railway and the London & Brighton Railway were brought concurrently to Parliament as both companies had to come to some agreement on the Croydon to Redhill section common to them both. The London & Brighton company was empowered to purchase the Croydon-Merstham section of the Grand Surrey Railway (the old CMG), but equally gave an option to the South Eastern Railway to purchase the Coulsdon to Red Hill section of its new line on completion. The London & Brighton Railway was thus responsible for constructing the line through Merstham, following a route determined by Sir John Rennie of London Bridge fame. South of East Croydon, the stations were "Godstone Road" (later Purley), "Stoats Nest" where the public road to Coulsdon was crossed, Merstham, Red Hill where Reigate Road provided access for Lord Somers, and so on. Lord Monson had been able to negotiate for a station at Merstham, over half a mile south of the present station, since Battlebridge farm was part of his estates. As the original Redhill station was also further south than its modern namesake, it was at Merstham that travellers would have to change between the two railways. If Jolliffe was still a proprietor of the CMG he would have been annoyed to find its initial asking price of £42,000 knocked down to £9,614 on arbitration in 1838. The horse-powered line was kept open only as long as it was needed to supply the contractors of the new railway.

Work on the new line was carried out at a tremendous pace, each section being given to a different contractor with its private army of navvies. The construction of Merstham tunnel, almost a mile long, went to the Thomas & William Hoof partnership (as evidenced on the Merstham gravestone of their fifty-year-old brother Henry, who died during the construction). A painting in Merstham's primary school records the pick, shovel and barrow intensity of the project, the sides of the cutting kept deliberately steep to save time and cost. Merstham's population of 713 was almost outnumbered by this horde of labourers whose reputation was already fearsome. According to the census taker these tent-dwellers were mainly from Derbyshire, Staffordshire and Yorkshire "and are the most uncultivated beings on earth". On pay days, doors and windows were locked up tight as drunken navvies roamed the village streets, cursing and fighting. In the absence of a police force, Jolliffe would rely on his yeomanry (the Bourbon regiment) to keep order in the area. Both winters of 1839/40 and 1840/41 were wet enough to delay progress, the sodden chalk spoil needing

Gatton House and Lake 1842

time to stabilise before earthworks could be trusted as secure. Although not fully complete, the line was opened from Croydon to Haywards Heath in July 1841, and from there to Brighton two months later. Before this final opening, the line's first accident happened near Hooley Lane when an inspector's train ran into a line of horse-pulled wagons full of earth from the works. Some wagons were smashed and the locomotive derailed. But in no time the railway was busy earning its keep. Merstham tunnel was initially whitewashed and illuminated by gas lights, as a result of concerns expressed by Parliament when first considering Sir John Rennie's plans. Merstham's first station was opened on 1st December 1841.

Unfortunately Lord Monson was not there to celebrate the occasion. He was only thirty-two when he died that October, childless and with his new estate still incomplete. He was buried in the churchyard of St Andrew's, Gatton, "in a simple stone mausoleum" of which only the base now exists. The tribute to him in the church was put there by his mother: "In the year of Christ 1834 this village church was rebuilt and ornamented at his sole charge; what was perished by premature decay, he restored; what was defaced by injudicious repair, he corrected; and rendered this house of prayer more befitting the honour and worship of Him the Almighty, Creator, Redeemer and Sanctifier". The Monson peerage and estates, including Gatton, now passed to his fourty-five-year-old cousin, William John Monson who shared his taste for Grand Tours. The sixth baron preferred, however, to bring up his family in the Monson ancestral home at Burton Hall in Lincolnshire and leave Gatton to the care of the Countess of Warwick. Within fifteen months of the Gatton funeral, there was a similar solemnity at St Katherine's for sixty-nine-year-old Hylton Jolliffe who had died at his London home on New Year's day 1843. It would seem both burials were carried out by Reverend J. Cecil Wynter, who, together with his curate Edward Greene, looked after Merstham parish as well as his Gatton living for quite some time, an interesting reversal of the present situation whereby Gatton falls under Merstham's rector.

By 1841 the agricultural depression was so bad that the Tories forced a vote of no confidence on the Whig administration. In the general election that followed Sir William Jolliffe was returned for Petersfield unopposed, Hector having retired. A new generation of Tories flocked to the Carlton Club, hoping for office, but Jolliffe had no more luck than his younger colleague, Disraeli. Although Sir Robert Peel brilliantly brought the economy back under control, in so doing he alienated most of his party who instinctively preferred protectionist to free trade policies. In the spirit of the Conservatives that allowed the Whig Liberals to take office in 1846, Jolliffe sided with the future Earl of Derby's protectionists against the Peelites. It was a period of fierce party conflict, with debates being frequently most acrimonious. The Speaker at this time was Charles Shaw Lefevre, whose dignity, temper and firmness had earned him this unenviable task which he was to hold for over thirty-three years.

The arrival of the railway continued to cause changes in Merstham. The toll road was largely rebuilt, albeit for a diminished coaching traffic, and several new buildings arose. The "Jolliffe Arms" was built on the improved road in front of the former "Hylton Arms Hotel", with Jolliffe cottages, a mini estate of terraced stone houses, between it and a lime works. "The Feathers" took on its curious bent shape at this time, while the gradient of School Hill was increased to take the new railway underneath. By the end of 1842 the South Eastern Railway had been opened from Red Hill to Ashford, so that four different railway companies operated to London Bridge, Merstham being the junction for two of them. The South Eastern took over control of the Red Hill to Coulsdon section from The London & Brighton, though not settling the terms of purchase until 1844. It was the South Eastern that closed Merstham station in October 1843 while it built a new interchange station at the present Redhill site, confusingly called "Reigate". Redhill as a town did not yet exist. Its embryo was "Warwick town", a cluster of houses south of Linkfield Lane under lease from the Countess of Warwick's Gatton estate. But apart from the new station, the only building East of this was the Philanthropic Farm School in 1849. The poor popularity of the Redhill area, before the arrival of the railway, can be ascribed to the workhouses of the Reigate Union of parishes (which included Merstham) having been built at both Shaw's Corner and on the site of the later Redhill General Hospital after the Poor Law Amendments of 1834. The Brighton line had closed its Reigate Road station so that the new station served both lines. Jolliffe must have missed his local station, for the South Eastern rebuilt Merstham station nearer the village, on its present site, in October 1844. The railway carried not only passengers but also their coaches and horses for use beyond the terminal.

Across the country the effect of the new railways was to give a massive boost to the economy. Locally its main impact was on Reigate, the east end of which began to develop with the 1849 branch line from "Reigate Junction" (ie Redhill) to the Great Western Railway at Reading, with "Reigate Town" station at its present Reigate site. Between 1851 and 1861 Reigate's population doubled to almost 10,000 (and its voting population increased from 350 to 700). Merstham had experienced this sudden growth rate with the advent of the Surrey Iron Railway a generation earlier, so that there was little extra growth in its population, still under 1,000, over this period. This can be

Merstham's mill, church & rail from an engraving for
the South Eastern Railways' guide book of 1858.

compared with Chipstead, still a non-railway parish at the
time, with only 500. Initially there were forty-five trains a
day going through Merstham, carrying many more, at
much less cost, and much more safely, than had the
highway coaches. Travel was not to be the only method of
broadening the mind. Both Gatton and Merstham were
provided with their first purpose-built School Houses to
provide elementary, and religious education to the villages.
It is also from this period that there was a growing number
of guide and history publications, usually reiterating earlier
descriptive texts. A common description of Merstham
House, first published in 1850, called it "an irregular
building, but surrounded by pleasing grounds; and its
general effect upon the eye is good. The house was much
improved a few years since under the direction of Mr
Knowles. With regard to comfort, the appartments are well
arranged, and elegantly furnished. The hall is handsome,
and connected by a flight of stone steps with the gallery,

which is also of stone; from which are the entrances to the principal bedrooms, etc. The mansion contains a few pictures; but the family portraits are at the seat of the present baronet's mother". Although the house is now but a memory to the older residents of Merstham, the Walker family in Reigate have some photographic plates that support this description. The best surviving work of T. R. Knowles locally is the tower of Kingswood Warren. Prints from engravings to illustrate such publications also survive. References to Gatton become scarce, however, following the death of the Countess of Warwick in 1852. Gatton continued to be administered by the sixth Baron Monson and his wife, Eliza, daughter of Edward Larken. In the south west, Nutwood Lodge was let to Lord William Fitzroy, while to the north, Upper Gatton was occupied from 1847 by John Currie Esquire, probably a nephew of the Mark Currie that had owned Upper Gatton between 1790 and 1796. To the south east, Pendell Court was inhabited by Charles Manning, brother of the future Cardinal.

Against the background of Continental revolution, the Whig administration again failed to maintain its majority against a coalition of Conservatives and Peelites, so that in February 1852 Queen Victoria asked Lord Derby to form a Conservative government. It was a difficult situation as the Conservatives owed their position to the divisions of their opponents and would always need an ally to command a majority in the House. Without the Peelites, Derby's ministry was composed almost entirely of men without experience of high office, the *Who, who administration* as it was called, after the Duke of Wellington's enquiry. Disraeli was appointed Chancellor of the Exchequer, Spencer Walpole the Home secretary. Sir William Jolliffe became Under-secretary of State for Home affairs. Appropriately his youngest son, born in January 1853, was named Spencer Jolliffe in tribute (the Walpoles owned Doggett's Farm next to Jolliffe's Chipstead estates). The following month Lord Stanley was discussing party matters with Disraeli: "Mackenzie has not given satisfaction as whipper-in. It was debated whether Stafford or Jolliffe should succeed. I strongly urged the latter. The wonder is that independent

Sir William Jolliffe, Bart., Secretary to the Treasury —
from a photograph by Herbert Watkins.

gentlemen will accept such a post".[17] But Jolliffe did, and became responsible for mustering the Tory faithful, outside as much as inside Parliament. In the general election that followed, the Conservatives gained over 100 seats, but with 310 members against 270 Whigs, 40 Peelites and 40 Irish Nationalists, they were as vulnerable as the recent Whig administration had been. Although admitting protectionist policies were out of date, the administration could not survive its first budget and by December the same year Jolliffe found himself out of government. His situation was uncomfortably similar to that of his grandfather in 1783.

Another similarity with his grandfather was how his heir had to prove himself in the major war of the time, and again in the Middle East. Luckily only two of Sir William's five surviving sons were old enough to be involved in the Crimean war. The eldest, Captain Hylton Jolliffe, was twenty-seven years old when his regiment, the Cold-stream Guards (the same as that of his late uncle Hylton), sailed for Gallipoli in February 1854. His brother, Lieutenant Hedworth Hylton Jolliffe, was twenty-four and with the 4th Light Dragoons, whose commander, Lord Paget, was related to Hedworth's mother. Hylton's young brother-in-law, Sir Henry Tyrwitt, was also there, with the Rifle Brigade. Captain Jolliffe survived the battle of the Alma in which the Guards were well involved, Lieutenant Jolliffe's light cavalry then chasing the routed Russians back towards Sebastopol. Two weeks later, on 4th October 1854, Captain Hylton Jolliffe died of cholera, the scourge that was to carry off considerably more of the allies than did enemy action. He left two infant girls, so that Lieutenant Hedworth Jolliffe was now the new heir. Three weeks later Hedworth himself was extremely lucky to escape death. For he was with his regiment in the famous charge of the Light Brigade of Balaklava. Half of the 4th Light Dragoons' senior officers were casualties. Of those unscathed, Lord Paget took over command of the Light Brigade from Lord Cardigan, Captain Low was promoted to command the remnants of the regiment, Captain Portal went on to publish one of the few sources of subsequent histories of the charge, and Lieutenant Jolliffe was promoted to Captain. The remnant of the Light Brigade was present at the Battle of Inkerman,

The Charge of the Light Brigade, 25th October 1854
A contemporary woodcut depicts the 11th Hussars and
4th Light Dragoons (Lt. Jolliffe) following the 17th
Lancers and 13th Light Dragoons through the Russian
guns.

which was largely an infantry affair, with the Guards
regiments losing a lot of their officers. With the Light
Brigade incapable of further active service, Lord Paget
returned to England, which caused a certain amount of
press criticism, Hedworth transferred into his brother's
regiment, the Coldstream Guards. While Paget felt obliged
to rejoin the Crimean staff in February 1855, it would seem
Hedworth was given leave to return home before the end of
the campaign, for he is later noted as a witness to the

Reverend J. Cecil Wynter's marriage to his second wife, Mary Cattley of Chipstead. Certainly Sir William moved quickly to realign the career of his next heir. One of his Conservative colleagues, Robert Tudway, had died in October, leaving vacant the Wells parliamentary seat that his family had held since 1760. In a contested by-election, Captain Hedworth Jolliffe of Merstham was duly elected as the new member for Wells in November 1855 (the other member for Wells was Sir William's opposite number, the Whig chief whip). In May 1856 he resigned his commission and two years later married Agnes Byng, a niece of Lord Paget, his former commanding officer. A commemorative plaque was put up to Captain Hylton Jolliffe in St Katharine's.

Palmerston still governed the country with his eloquent appeals to patriotic fervour, handling with care the incidents in Persia, China and India. But concern for Reform, checked by War, could no longer be delayed. A curious combination of Russell's Whigs, Gladstone's Peelites and pacifist Radicals were prepared to put the Conservatives in to get Palmerston out. In the 1857 elections, the Jolliffes of Merstham, father and son, took their Petersfield and Wells seats unopposed. The Reigate seat was won by William Hackblock, a retired City banker and ardent reformer who lived at "The Rock", Reigate Hill. When he died in January 1858, Lord Monson's eldest son, William, Hedworth's contemporary but "of thoroughly Liberal opinions", contested Reigate. He came third with only twenty-two per cent of the by-election vote. Within months the victor was promoted to high office in India, giving William Monson another chance. In October 1858 Monson gained Reigate, the seat of his ancestor over 200 years previously, though only by 225 votes to 210 and by using as much bribery as the opposition! Nevertheless, for both Gatton and Merstham, the pattern of the gentry had been re-established: Eldest sons were in Parliament, second sons in the army. Young Sydney Jolliffe took on a military career where Hedworth left off, though with the 29th Foot, while John Monson had already seen active service with the 52nd Foot in the Indian Mutiny campaign.

Once again Lord Derby formed a government without a

majority in the Commons. Disraeli and Walpole were again Chancellor of the Exchequer and Home Secretary respectively, while Sir William Jolliffe became Parliamentary Secretary to the Treasury, the official title of his chief whip position. It was to be no easy task, for Lord Derby felt obliged to offer electoral reform and such was anathema to most of his Conservative party. Without the backing of key members such as Walpole, Jolliffe had little hope of mustering enough support to defeat the opposition and Lord Derby's Reform Bill failed by 291 to 330 votes in March 1859. Instead of resigning, Derby decided to fight a general election. It fell upon Jolliffe as chief whip to organise the extra, as well as intra, parliamentary party support. It is thus a tribute to him that, as a result of the election, the Conservatives again commanded over 300 seats, similar to their 1853 achievement. It forced Palmerston and Russell to settle their differences and form a united, Liberal, coalition. Only then, in June, could they give the Derby administration the necessary vote of no confidence, it being carried by 323 to 310. Once more, after only a few but hectic months, the Conservatives were out of office. Sir William Jolliffe's effort was appreciated, however, so that he not only received a testimonial in plate for his services as whip, but was also made a Privy Councillor the same month. Sir William was a professional politician, "in a peculiar way, for many years a prominent member of the House of Commons", and his hopes of a peerage were known to his colleagues. Having yet again to assume the role of the opposition must have been frustrating though it allowed him more time to run his estates. On 8th March 1864 the elderly Sir William caused a most unfortunate accident: "He was shooting rabbits near a chalkpit, when a boy put his head out at the moment of firing, received the charge, and died that night. Jolliffe is said to be much distressed".[7]

St Katharine's was "entirely restored" in 1861, the local builder concerned being allowed to remove virtually all of the screen-work ("little less than a disaster" in the opinion of Merstham's post-Victorian critic, Llewellyn Williams ARIBA, Paxton Watson's contemporary), at a cost of some £900. Sir William, his rector Reverend John Manley, and George Lyall of the Bank of England were the main contributors; surprisingly the other major contributions came from the residents of Nutfield Priory, then owned by Henry Gurney, a cadet of a remarkable Norfolk family of Quaker bankers. In each generation, a Gurney had married a Birkbeck, and it was Edward Birkbeck, brother-in-law of Henry Gurney, who married Lord Hylton's youngest daughter, Mary, in 1865. The following year the Gurney's bank, which had been the greatest discount house in the world, went dramatically bankrupt with debts of £11 million. Prudently the partners had converted the business to a joint stock company some months earlier, thus limiting their personal loss. Henry Gurney sold Nutfield Priory and moved to Nutwood Lodge in the south west corner of the new Lord Monson's Gatton estate. Edward Birkbeck, who seems not to have been involved in the affair, stayed at his Norfolk home, and in due course was knighted for his work as Chairman of the Royal National Lifeboat Institute.

Lord Palmerston's new, broad based, Liberal administration was characterised by six years of constant disturbance abroad but political inactivity at home. Only after his death was electoral reform allowed to be brought before Parliament in 1866, whereupon it caused sufficient divisions in the Liberal party for Lord Derby to be asked for a third time to form a government with only a minority in the House of Commons. This time he brought Jolliffe to the Upper House, Sir William becoming Baron Hylton of Hylton and Petersfield (his Petersfield seat was taken unopposed by a Liberal, William Nicholson). William Monson had also left the Commons for the Lords following the death of his father in 1862, his Reigate seat going to another Liberal, William Leveson Gower of Titsey Park. In the 1865 general election one of Monson's brothers (thirty-one-year-old Edmund, later a successful diplomat) had contested Reigate, lost and lodged an appeal. The commissioners brought in to uncover Reigate's sorry tale of bribery and corruption in every election since 1857, started their task at a time of feverish concern for reform. For, with increased prosperity and less concern about revolution, Reform was no longer anathema to the Conservatives. Indeed, the growth of the new towns and the need to address the disparity of the existing franchise qualifications made it an obvious cause for Lord

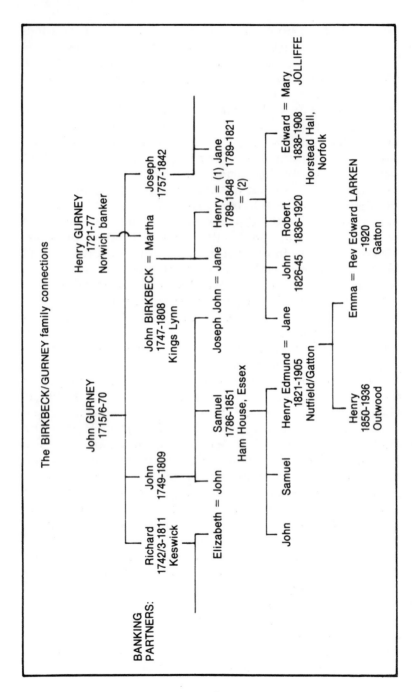

The BIRKBECK/GURNEY family connections

Derby's third administration to take up.

In July 1867, while the London mobs were flocking to Hyde Park to the banner of the Reform League, Merstham was visited by a large group of "eminent persons, including leaders in the mining and quarrying industries, road construction and waterworks". The Peters family had taken over the Merstham quarry business from the Halls a few years earlier (James Hall moving to Horley) and it was presumably Mr Peters who invited the thirty-four-year-old Swede, Alfred Nobel, to demonstrate his new, safer, form of nitro-glycerine. Nitro-glycerine was then the widely used blasting material, and was as dangerous to handle then as it is now: In Newcastle that December, seven were blown up in a typical handling disaster. Alfred Nobel had found the addition of kieselguhr (silicious earth) stablised the explosive fluid, and it was this new compound, called "dynamite", that was tried and approved at Merstham quarries. Alfred Nobel went on from this to build a huge armaments fortune which ironically funded the Peace Prize that still bears his name. The Peters family stayed at Quarry Dean Farm until the 1930s. The quarry has largely disappeared under the M23. There is no monument to this first demonstration of dynamite by its inventor.

The success of the Derby administration in finally enacting a Reform bill lies largely with the Commons, and especially Derby's lieutenant there, Disraeli. As Lord Hylton, William had little interest in the precise terms of reform of elections to the Lower House; as one of the members for Wells, the Honorable Hedworth found his seat disenfranchised by his own party. Reigate similarly was deprived of its seat and merged with a County Division. The Reform Act required the dissolution of Parliament, and the election in 1868 gave Gladstone's Liberals an overwhelming majority, thus ending another brief period of Conservative government. Hedworth did not share his father's interest in party politics and made no further effort to stand for Parliament, even for Petersfield where Nicholson fought off a challenge from a fellow Liberal. Lord Hylton's enthusiasm must also have waned, for he was only a year younger than his leader, Lord Derby, who had died in 1869 after a long illness. He spent the remaining years of his life

Merstham House, the seat of Lord Hylton.

at Merstham with his second wife, the widow of the Earl of
Ilchester. The Jolliffes' dining companions would like as
not be the Kennards of Upper Gatton Park, the Aubertins
of Chipstead's Rectory at Mugswell, the Wynters of
the Rectory, the Roffeys of the Grange, the Mangles of
Pendell Court or the Fieldens at the rebuilt Nutfield Priory.
When not visiting Merstham, Hedworth spent his time at
his London house, near Hyde Park, enjoying the company
of his friends at the Carlton, White's, and Turf Clubs.
Whether with his father in the country or his friends
in town, the topics of conversation would have included
the effect of the long drought of '70, the Education Act
which was the greatest enactment of State intervention yet,
the poor health of the Prince of Wales and the amazing outcome of the Franco-Prussian war. In common with other
military landowners, Hedworth would have discussed
Chesney's influential pamphlet, *The Battle of Dorking* which
cast doubts about Britain's ability to resist a German
invasion, and argued long over Cardwell's subsequent
reforms of the Army system that had so much dominated his

own formative youth. In 1872 Hedworth took advantage of the still somewhat novel civil divorce proceedings to become legally separated from his wife. His son, George, and daughter, Agatha, were only ten and nine at the time.

Gatton was at this time let by Lord Monson to Robert McCalmont, formerly of Belfast. As with many an Ulster Scots family, the McCalmonts produced a number of good army officers. Robert, however, did not spend long enough in the Artillery to achieve a rank worth mentioning and must be the most anonymous gentleman to reside at Gatton. His wife, Margaret, was a younger sister of another Ulster Scot, Hugh McCalmont Cairns, the Lord Chancellor. This is why Cairns was "a familiar figure in the parish". Ten years older than Robert, and Hedworth, Hugh Cairns had been elevated to the peerage at the same time as Sir William Jolliffe and was Lord Chancellor in Disraeli's administrations, being leader of the party in the Lords in the meantime. More respected than popular, Lord Cairns suffered from poor health and would have found his sister's Gatton home a convenient haven.

By 1874 Gladstone's ministry had accomplished more than expected of it, but in doing so had excited much opposition. His appeal to the electorate that year with the bait of a promised repeal of income tax, was seen for the bribe it was. Hedworth's brother, Sydney, took the opportunity to challenge Nicholson at Petersfield and won by 372 to 361 votes, very much in line with the swing to the Conservatives nationally. Nicholson's petition was dismissed and another Jolliffe joined Disraeli in victory. Sydney was to maintain the family seat until Gladstone once more swept the Liberals to power in 1880, when Nicholson outvoted Jolliffe by 406 to 320. Well before then, however, on 1st June 1876, Lord Hylton died. He was seventy-five and had lived to see the local changes initiated by his father and uncle brought to fruition. He had achieved the family ambition to resurrect the Hylton barony and had a grandson, George, to maintain it. Certainly forty-seven-year-old Hedworth inherited secure titles and estates, but, as one of the heros of the Light Brigade, he had been left no challenge, and in turn leaves no mark on the next two decades of late Victorian Merstham.

I O

MUSTARD AND BOVRIL
1878-1913

Compared to the 'hungry forties', the 1880s were prosperous indeed. Nowhere was this more evident than in the growing railway towns such as Redhill. With Merstham, Gatton and Reigate owned by the Lords Hylton, Monson and Somers, the local railway-induced development was largely confined to the marshy area south of Linkfield Lane. Thus Reigate's Eastern ward rapidly established a separate, Redhill, character, with its own schools and churches, gas and water companies (with a reservoir at the top of Shepherds Hill), and the sort of standardised red brick housing that was so widespread that a reaction against this period of architecture was inevitable. Only recently have the merits of some of these buildings been recognised. Initially Hedworth was able to resist the pressure for property development and it was the small landowners of the parish who provided the appropriate plots for development. Merstham's mid-Victorian buildings were the singular houses of The Gables in Quality Street, Oakley House and Coppice Lea off the Bletchingley Road. Oakley, for example, was a typical gentleman's house built for Percy Pelly, the youngest son of the late governor of the Bank of England, and of the Hudsons Bay Company at the time of its exploration for a North West Passage. Percy had married Eliza Rigge of Belmont Castle and moved to Merstham for a house and environs appropriate to his station in life. Coppice Lea was built in the grounds in 1881 for the eldest son, Percy John, after his marriage to Florence Butler from Elmore, Chipstead. As expected at that time, the family would be outnumbered by the number of staff they employed. Only a minority of the villagers relied on the land for a living. From this period there was a steady decline in British agriculture, as the Victorian manufacturer and merchant fed more cheaply with cereals from America and frozen meat from Australasia, imported on the same British steam-ships that exported his products. At the same time the accepted code of conduct of the county aristocracy that is associated with the Victorian era, was already being eroded by the less-comfortable aspects of democracy and bureaucracy espoused by the newly-educated generation.

It can be assumed that the owners of Merstham and Gatton were as remote from the new intellectual liberality as they were from their Surrey tenants. Hedworth, the second Baron Hylton, was a natural conservative, at home in the London-club and country-house gatherings of yesterday's establishment. A year after the death of his former wife in 1878, he married the widow of the Earl of Dunraven in Rome. Of his two children, Agatha was the first to marry. She was twenty-two when she married Ailwyn Edward Fellowes in 1886. The following year her father-in-law, already suffering from a serious illness, was granted a peerage, one of eight created for the Jubilee. He died five months later, whereupon Agatha's brother-in-law became Lord De Ramsey. Hedworth's contemporary, the seventh Baron Monson, had been a member of the Queen's household since 1874, though still a Liberal, supporting Gladstone as one of the Speakers to the House of Lords, and been rewarded by being made a viscount in 1886. Tactfully, he chose not to resurrect the Monson viscountcy of his regicide ancestor, but chose instead a name from the same period of his family's history, Oxenbridge. Lord Oxenbridge, then, would have found his Lincoln home often inconvenient as a base from which to carry out his official duties. Gatton clearly held no appeal for him, for he decided to sell his Gatton estates and buy Chart Lodge, Sevenoaks. First though, he transferred the tomb of the fifth baron and his mother, the Countess of Warwick, to the Monson chapel in Burton-by-Lincoln. The rector there was a relation of his, probably an uncle, the Reverend Edmund Larken, whose claim to infamy was to be 'the first clergyman to wear a beard in the pulpit'. He is not to be confused with a younger relative, also Reverend Edmund Larken, who was appointed rector of Gatton by Monson following seventy-year-old Wynter's death in 1877, and who married one of his parishoners, Henry Gurney's daughter, Emma, in 1881. The father of Gatton's young rector was Metcalf Larken of the Sudan Civil Service so the kinship with his namesake was not too close.

Not only in Merstham and Gatton, but also in Reigate was there considerable anxiety that Gatton would become another Redhill. In the event it was only by a matter of £200 out of £82,000 that a gentleman of means secured the estate against a development syndicate in 1888. Once again Gatton was to have a resident owner, and the estate workers turned out with interest to view Mr Jeremiah Colman, his wife Mary, and their infant son, also called Jeremiah. Mr Colman was only twenty-nine when he bought Gatton, but he came with all the authority of a senior member of the established firm of J & J Colman, mustard, starch and blue manufacturers of Cannon Street in the City. He was very much part of the City establishment, an alderman of the Skinners Livery Company, and occasional chairman of Commercial Union, the insurance company of which his father had been a co-founder. He was High Sheriff of Surrey for 1893 and the following year he took over the chairmanship of J & J Colman from his sixty-four-year-old cousin, Jeremiah James Colman, Liberal member of Parliament for Norwich and breeder of red-polled cattle. It was probably through his cousin's influence that Gatton came to be well stocked with Highland cattle and pedigree Shorthorns, while the Gatton flock of Southdown sheep were soon winning awards up and down the country. They also shared an interest in horticulture and Gatton soon boasted excellent gardens, including rock, rose and Japanese gardens, rivalling the Wiggey Homestead gardens run by Richard Trower of Battlebridge House. Colman's speciality, though, was orchids, and apart from gaining a crop of awards, he also published *Hybridisation of Orchids* for private circulation. The house was also improved, Monson's marble hall being wrapped round with the large portico that still dominates the South front. Between Monson and Colman, Gatton became 'the best example in the country of what might be called Canova architecture', though sadly so little survives. The house was soon filled with appropriate furniture, statues, and paintings, including works by Turner (*Lucerne from the Walls*, now in the Lady Lever Art Gallery, Port Sunlight), Watts and Burne Jones, as well as a Raphael. As Hope Moncrieff later wrote: 'Gatton passed into the hands of a gentleman who boasts how he made his money from the mustard people superfluously leave on their plates, and of whom his Redhill neighbours cause to think that he spends it with like liberty' (though the boast was actually that of his father).

Although not in the same league, another City merchant came out to rural Merstham at this time. William Grieve built a suitable house for his family at Gatton Point called 'Ringwood'. Grieve was a Scotsman from Dalbeattie and chairman of Bulloch Bros & Co. Ltd. (later part of the Inchcape group), Burma merchants and shipping agents, specialising in rice. The Grieves were typical of the Victorian merchant classes, recently rich, solid supporters of Gladstone, and self-taught through experience in enterprises where the risk/reward factors were finely balanced. Ring-wood must have been just within Merstham's boundary as the Grieves buried one of their young daughters at St Katharine's, and gave the church its sixth bell in her memory. From their well-sited house the Grieve family would have had a grandstand view of the first Brighton run on 14th November 1896, when some fifty new fangled motor cars celebrated their freedom to travel at twelve mph on the public roads! It was to be thirty years before the run was repeated in what by then were vintage cars. The then annual repetition developed into the international event that Merstham residents have come to expect each November.

While there was no increase in the 240 parishioners that maintained, and were maintained by, Gatton, the population of Merstham was to double to 2,000 in the next decade.

Reverend and Mrs Woodhouse and daughters

The 'expansive eighties' may have been replaced by what was later called the 'naughty nineties', but it was also a period of almost universal church attendance. St Katharine's new rector in 1894, Reverend R. Woodhouse from Bromley, was typical of the new generation of well educated clergymen, publishing, during his time at Merstham, his *Life of Cardinal Morton* (Sir Thomas More's mentor), *The Poetical Works of James Woodhouse* (the Georgian 'poetic shoemaker') and *Merstham Parish Registers 1538-1812*. But he was not purely an academic. Within a year he had convinced the residents of the need for a Mission Room in the growing Southern section of the parish, probably to counter the growing nonconformist influence of Redhill, and a site was donated on Nutfield Road. Princess Frederika of Hanover laid the foundation stone in 1897 of what was to become All Saints Church, at a cost of only £2,300. The separate parish of South Merstham was formed (and the boundary between Merstham and Gatton parishes rearranged) in 1899 with Reverend William London its first vicar. By then the core of the new parish was the development of buildings between Albury and Battlebridge farms, on Manor, Endsleigh and Southcote Roads, their Albert service road and the adjacent part of Nutfield Road. Apart from the obvious pressure this growth put on the village infrastructure, such as the school house, the fire station, drainage, etc, there was an added bonus of a new source of cricketers. For under John Shuter, Surrey had been county champions for six successive seasons (a decade before Jack Hobbs), and with this inspiration Merstham's new cricket club was never short of good quality volunteers. The main cricket supporter locally was Jeremiah Colman himself, whose father had been one of eleven brothers who played as a team in Norfolk half a century earlier. He was a member of the SCC and organised several matches at Gatton.

For fifty years the London, Brighton & South Coast Railway had competed with the South Eastern Railway, with a rivalry that may have kept fares low, but otherwise led to some strange situations. For example, Lord Hylton's neighbour, H. Cosmo Bonsor of Watney's, had failed to get sufficient support for an extension of the L B & S C Epsom branch line to his home at Kingswood Warren and so looked for a new branch line to run through Chipstead Bottom to Kingswood. The South Eastern Railway was delighted to take the opportunity to strike at the heart of L B & S C territory with its profitable Epsom Races traffic, and 'sold' Bonsor a place on its board in exchange for sponsoring the new branch line to Kingswood. Cosmo Bonsor became chairman of the South Eastern Railway within months of the opening of this 'Director's line' and soon extended it to Tattenham Corner. Another aspect of the railway companies' rivalry that effected Merstham was one company deliberately scheduling a slow stopping train just ahead of its rival company's express! In 1894 the situation was improved with an Act that enabled double tracks from Croydon to Purley and a new by-pass line from Stoat's Nest (Coulsdon South) to Earlswood, just South of Redhill. At Merstham a new tunnel was required under Shepherds Hill. It was a difficult task for the engineers, given the Southern end was to run through the old quarries to the West of the Peters' Greystone Lime Works. Here Merstham's labyrinth of medieval workings was only explored by the foolhardy and included such dangers as 'the undisturbed accumulation of gas given off by the limestone rock'. The stretch of track is still known locally as the Quarry Line. Throughout 1896 Merstham was once again a construction site, but the work was more automated than before: 'Every now and again steam-navvies are to be seen grabbing up great buckets of dirt and dropping them into waiting trucks, each doing the work of twenty men and giving employment but to two'. Where the cutting sliced through Rockshaw Road (then 'nothing more than a cart track'), the Durrant windmill which was owned by the Stacey family at the time, had to be demolished. The spindle, grindstones and beams were then used to make a splendid lychgate for St Katharine's. Perhaps this was the time of a similar removal and rebuilding of the old dove-cot, reputedly fourteenth century, behind Wellhead, where it remains a landmark despite being split by a falling tree in the gales of January 1990 and subsequently restored. The quarry line went on past the new occupants of Albury manor and divided historic Battlebridge house from its farm, another indication of how unimportant agriculture had become compared to the railways. On the other hand the railways employed their own medical officers and it was one such, Dr Henry Crickitt, who stayed on in Merstham, becoming the village's first general practitioner.

Hedworth had been born in Merstham at a time when railways meant an occasional horse-drawn line of waggons. With his Surrey estate being hemmed in by sooty engines and red-brick developments, one can understand his dwindling interest in it, though Merstham remained his principal seat in official documents. It was still convenient for occasional house parties or seasonal shoots at Cold Roast and Boors Green Farms on Harps Oak Lane but, for hunting and the open country, Ammerdown had more to offer. His son, George, was in the diplomatic service until the Home Rule bill signalled the end of the Liberal Party's control of Parliament. This gave thirty-three-year-old George his opportunity to resume the family tradition and he succeeded in gaining the Wells division of Somerset in the swing to the Unionists in the 1895 elections. The following year he married Lady Alice Hervey, daughter of the Marquess of Bristol, and clearly preferred the tranquillity of Ammerdown to the bustle of Merstham. When Hedworth died at Ammerdown on 31st October 1899 (and was buried in the family vault at St Katharine's), George inherited an estate of over 10,000 acres, of which 4,400 was in Surrey, 4,300 was in Somerset, and 1,300 was in Hampshire. In due course he rationalised this by selling the Petersfield estate to his uncle, Sydney, and let the Merstham estate to Mr Andrew Walker.

Andrew Walker was another City Scotsman, ten years older than William Grieve. Although both were a generation older than Colman, Walker's wealth came, like that of Colman, from a modest foodstuff that remains a household name to this day. John Lawson Johnston had invented Bovril, the 'beef tea' concoction, in 1889 and Andrew Walker had helped in the 1896 company reconstruction that made it so successful. By the turn of the century Andrew was in his sixties but still Managing Director of Bovril Ltd., sharing the board with his second son, Douglas, two Lawson Johnstons and an appropriate peer for chairman. The London factory of Bovril was on the northern edge of the City, with its own electricity supply and its own artesian well. This insularity in corporate matters is in keeping with Walker's establishment at Merstham. In contrast to the Colmans, the Walkers seem to have avoided all community groups and modestly enjoyed merely the company of their own family (there seem to have been at least nine children: Helen later Mrs Puckle, Andrew, Douglas, Hector, Margaret, Rosamund later Mrs Nicholson, Grace later Mrs Nicholson and then the second Mrs Puckle, Mary and Alan). At least Merstham House was once more fully occupied and operational.

The turn of the century was otherwise marked by the South African War, Lord Hylton's three Petersfield cousins were all involved, the eldest John Jolliffe, being killed at Paardeberg. In Merstham, only the Roffeys of The Grange appear to have been involved so far in military affairs. George Roffey had two sons. The eldest, Walter, had just come out of the army to marry Constance Lawrence in 1897, but his younger brother, Captain Harold Roffey of the Lancashire Fusiliers, who had already seen action on

India's North West frontier, served throughout the Boer War, returning to Merstham in a new century and to a new monarch.

The coronation of Edward VII was due on 26th June 1902. He fell ill two days before, causing the national festivities to be postponed. Not in Merstham: On 26th June virtually the entire parish celebrated with a lunch for 1,000 adults and a tea for 600 children. 'Sports were indulged in', noted the rector. Generally the main entertainment continued to be the theatre, and there was no greater concentration of theatres than in London's West End. Apart from Gilbert & Sullivan, comedy was favourite. The principal light comedian of the Gaity Company was young Seymour Hicks. In 1895 Ellaline Terriss joined the company. They were both the same age (twenty-four), had been professionally acting since they were sixteen, and were both born on small islands — Seymour at St Helier on Jersey, Ellaline at the Ship Hotel in the Falklands. They were soon married and taking the lead roles in such successes as *The Circus Girl*, during which Ellaline lost first her baby child, then her father, the actor William Terriss, who was stabbed by a madman. By the turn of the century they were at the Vaudeville Theatre, where in 1902 they played the leading roles in J. M. Barrie's successful play, *Quality Street*, which in terms of popularity came between *The Gondoliers* and *The Pirates of Penzance*. It was soon afterwards that the couple moved from Middlesex to the Old Forge just outside Lord Hylton's gates in Merstham, causing the comment: 'Ah, now all the *quality* live here'! The name stuck and since then this section of the old High Street has been called Quality Street. Apart from acting, Seymour also wrote plays (sixty-four in all) and books (seven, mainly on acting) and ran a couple of theatres. He did several tours of America with Ellaline, and had a well-deserved reputation for a 'lightning quick' wit, on and off the stage. As Macqueen Pope wrote in 1949, 'Young playgoers of today can have no idea at all of the tremendous power of Seymour Hicks, master of all the trades of the theatre, of his hold on the public, his tremendous zest, wit and versatility'.

Another resident of Quality Street was Mr Paxton Watson, a neo-Tudor architect whose main commission had

Ellaline Terriss and Seymour Hicks

been from Whitaker Wright (who was also to commission Lutyens) for Witley Park. It has since been demolished, but his District Council Offices and Moor Park work in Farnham still survive. The houses on the other side of the road from Merstham Grange, including the new Primary School, were built to his designs. 'Rockwood' was bought by young Peter Stephens of Thomas Stephens & Sons, an established City insurance broking firm, following his marriage to Lottie Simpson of Wray Park in 1902. Here can be seen the semi-circular topped, projecting, leaded windows peculiar to so many of Merstham's Edwardian buildings, and which act as Paxton Watson's local trade mark. Watson bought and rebuilt The Barn in 1902 and the Manor House/Court Cottage next door (in 1905 for his sister which was used in the inter-war film *When Winter Comes*). In 1903 Hilaire Belloc retraced the Pilgrims Way and found the likely route 'utterly lost in this mass of modern things, roads, railways, and cuttings, which we found just after Merstham church. We walked along the road that leads to

Rockshaw, and along which certain new villas have been built'. His modern counterpart can more easily follow the North Downs Way along Rockshaw Road past those same 'villas' with their Watson windows. Albury Edge was the first to be built on this road and remains Watson's best local example. It was built for R. Percy Sellon who at the time was a thirty-six-year-old director of Otis Elevators, twenty-five different traction and electrical supply companies and Managing Director of Johnson Matthey & Co., the London bullion dealers. According to Sir Harry Renwick, Percy was well read, modest and had a strong sense of duty; attributes, one suspects, that were more common in an entrepreneur then than now. Other houses on the south side soon followed, one of the less ornate, Clavadel, being built for Henry Nicholson, for twenty years a City solicitor and at that time Clerk to the Commissioners of Taxes. By now the economics of labour were such that new houses were built on the assumption that there would be less staff than family. The bottom of Church Hill was developed at the same time and with the same style of windows, the Church swopping land with Lord Hylton for the Verger's Cottage in 1906. Paxton Watson went on to oversee the restoration work to St Katharine's in 1909, the same year that a Methodist chapel was built in South Merstham, before moving from Barn House, Quality Street to Picket Wood, Rockshaw Road.

Merstham's new elementary school was just in time for the 1902 Education Act which transferred responsibility from the School Boards to the local councils. Gatton's primary -school, which dates from Monson's building programme of 1840, was closed briefly until Colman enlarged it to council specifications. At the time of writing, the old schoolroom at Gatton retains its Edwardian character with Jeremiah Colman's wall map still rolled up high on the wall (when the world was largely coloured British pink), as if at any moment children in pinafores and laced leather boots would return! Gatton's population remained much the same, but with some new faces: Reverend A. G. Rogers had come late to the priesthood, having travelled extensively in South America and the West Indies before being ordained in 1891 aged thirty-four. The

Reverend Rogers

retirement of Edmund Larken in 1894 provided him with his first, and indeed only, living of his own. Larken's father-in-law, Henry Gurney, died in 1905, to be succeeded at Nutwood Lodge by a cadet branch of another old Lincolnshire family: Captain Charles Jarvis was only thirty, son of the vicar of Doncaster when he arrived at Gatton, his senior cousins making it unlikely at this stage that he would inherit the ancestral seat of Doddington Hall. Charles had served with some distinction with the Yorkshire Regiment in the Boer War, and had also been at Paardeberg with young Jolliffe. He then retired from the regular army and married Captain Johnston-Stewart's widow, Helen Hunter-Blair, before arriving at Nutwood Lodge. Upper Gatton was occupied by a Mr Alfred Benson during this period.

The new families in Merstham and Gatton ostensibly lived with a degree of ease and stability that generations of wealth creation had led them to expect. Certainly there was mounting pressure for political and social reform at home, coupled with increasing competition from Germany and the States in trade overseas. But little of this was evident to a Surrey landowner (though Mrs Stephens of Rockwood and Miss Maud Roffey of the Grange were active suffragettes). Especially in the light of what was to come, it is difficult not to view the Edwardian decade through a romantic haze, as a period of comfortable elegance, with Colman organising his private cricket matches, Roffey his shooting parties, and Woodhouse his parish. True, the menace from Germany had resulted in a chain of forts along the North Downs, including one at Reigate Hill (which at £11,000 had cost almost five times as much as All Saints) and another beside the reservoir on Shepherds Hill, but concern was generally half-hearted. On a personal level, Sir Edward Birkbeck was one of those saved after a collision between a German motor torpedo boat and a British steamer in June 1902. Tragedies occurred for example: Late on the night of Sunday 24th September 1905, the mutilated body of a twenty-one-year-old girl was found in Merstham tunnel. The suicide, as was first thought, was taken to the Feathers where a more careful examination by Dr Crickitt made it obvious that she had been gagged and thrown from the down train. The girl was Mary Money, a bookkeeper from Wandsworth, who had not told anyone where she was going nor whom she intended to meet. The 'Merstham Tunnel Mystery' achieved a great deal of lurid publicity ('On the side of the tunnel were marks of her hands . . .') but remained unsolved. It was re-examined recently by the author, Jonathan Goodman, whose sympathy is limited by the suspicion that she delighted in dangerous deceptions.

The new Liberal government took a different approach to the German menace. Lord Haldane decided in 1907 that the North Downs defences could be sold, and part of Reigate Hill fort eventually fell to the Boy Scouts. Baden-Powell, the hero of Mafeking, had started the movement in 1907, and within a couple of years it had attracted over 100,000 members. It is not surprising that it was well represented locally, for when the formal Boy Scouts Association was established, its first Vice President was the recently knighted Sir Jeremiah Colman. Although Jeremiah's late uncle had refused a baronetcy years earlier, it was not until the return of the Liberals under Asquith that Jeremiah was offered the same honour in 1907. Lord Haldane's more important measure, however, was the establishment, in 1908, of a Territorial army based on the old volunteer forces. The new battalions were related to the regular ones. For example both the Royal West Surrey and the East Surrey regiments were allocated two Territorial battallions each. Despite their names, the Royal West Surrey recruited from, and were based, right across the rural county as far East as Lingfield, while the East Surrey was associated with the suburban part of the county, most of which had become part of London on the creation of that county in 1888. True to their family origins, Captain Jarvis looked after the Lincolnshire's territorial battalion, while the eldest of Grieve's three sons joined the Cameron Highlanders' territorial battalion.

The Liberals were equally generous with health care. For half a century Earlswood had been the only local asylum. Suddenly the Surrey hills became the favoured location for such institutions with the London asylum at Banstead, the Metropolitan at Caterham, the London County at Coulsdon and then the Surrey County at Netherne. Netherne Hospital was built in what was then Merstham parish in

1907/9 at a cost of £300,000 for a maximum of 1,480 mentally ill patients. By the 1911 census it had 950 inmates. With these excluded, Merstham had a population of 2,558. Woodhouse records that there were only ten motor cars in the whole village at this time. Bicycles were at their most popular during the Edwardian period, and represented the only common use of the pneumatic tyre. Apparently the first trial of a luxury motor bus with such tyres, the Charron Pullman, took place in Merstham (which may explain why Hicks' fellow comedian, Fred Karno, came to order one for his theatrical company in 1910), but it was not until 1911 that Merstham got its first regular, Leyland, motor bus route to Redhill from the new East Surrey Traction Co. Two years later it was opposition from the East Surrey that ensured that the powerful London General Omnibus Co. took its new Sunday excursion route from Stockwell to no further than the Feathers Hotel at Merstham. It caused some resentment from locals that rural Merstham should be so invaded by Londoners.

In two decades the population of Merstham had trebled. Of those with which this history is concerned, Andrew Walker was the eldest. In 1913, at seventy-five, he finally relinquished his post as Managing Director of Bovril in favour of his thirty-eight-year-old son, Douglas. Both Captain Harold Roffey of the Lancashire Fusiliers and Captain Charles Jarvis of the Lincolnshire Regiment were also thirty-eight that year. The new territorial arm was represented by Charles Grieve of the Gordon Highlanders, while twenty-seven-year-old Jeremiah Colman, as a justice of the peace, was a co-opted member of the Sussex Territorial Reserve. In another handover from one generation to the next, Dr Crickitt sold his practice in the High Street to his Scottish stepson, young Dr Walter Weir. In 1911 Walter met and married Ruth, the daughter of Reverend George Bell, while doing a locum in the Midlands. A John Bell, possibly a brother, bought one of the new houses in Rockshaw Road and called it 'As You Like It'. Clearly few did, for the name has not survived. The Rector of Gatton also lived on Rockshaw Road then, at a house named after his first appointment as curate to Kingsdown, Sevenoaks. Mr Rogers had two sons, the eldest being the same age as the only son of Merstham's rector. Both were young officers of twenty-two in 1913: R. Courtney Woodhouse had been commissioned in 1911 and, possibly influenced by Roffey, if not Kipling, joined the Indian Frontier Force that year. Wilfred Rogers was a year his junior in the Royal Field Artillery. The other fated members of this generation include the younger Grieves of Ringwood, the Stacey's of Walden, Lamaison of Worsted Green, and sixteen-year-old Gervaise Peters of Quarry Dean. For once, and in contrast to the situation at the time of the Napoleonic and Crimean wars, the Jolliffe boys, William and Thomas, were too young to be caught up in the initial call to arms, though their cousin, Agatha Fellowes' four boys, had already joined either the army or the navy. This was an educated generation, full of confidence, purpose and promise.

II

ALL CHANGE
1914-1948

Although there has since been a second World War, the first
was the Great War that divided what is considered modern
from what went before. For those who lived through this
period, it was, as J. B. Priestley put it, as if they 'suddenly
saw a great jagged crack in the looking-glass' and nothing
could ever be looked at in the same way again. But initially
there was more confidence than concern. In military terms,
Britain was not well prepared, having one of the smallest
armies in Europe. Yet, as previously noted, it was well
represented in Merstham and Gatton. Both Wilfred Rogers
and Harold Roffey were in the initial expeditionary force
and took part in the retreat from Mons, Roffey being
wounded in the process. The wounded who were ferried
back to England recuperated in Voluntary Aid Detach-
ments, often private houses volunteered for the purpose.
Merstham's VAD was Chaldon Rise on Rockshaw Road
with Walter Weir as its medical officer. Kitchener's new
army of volunteers was rapidly raised to bolster the thin line
across Flanders. The youngest Grieve boy had only just got
married, but left his wife at Ringwood to join his brothers
in the army. He had no sooner been commissioned into the
Middlesex Regiment than he was killed at Ypres on St
Valentine's day, 1915. His son was born a few weeks later.
The death the following month of seventy-seven-year-old
Andrew Walker would have been a much less emotive

event. Gradually the effects of the war became more obvious. Horses were requisitioned, pasture turned into vegetable patches and the younger men disappeared. Gervaise Peters joined the Buffs in India, L.W.H. Lamaison went into the Royal Warwickshires, Philip Rogers joined the Navy and John Stacey eventually ended up with the Flying Corps. Even Walter Roffey joined his younger brother's regiment and was soon posted to the Ministry of Food, while Walter Weir, after the birth of his son Christopher in 1916, joined the RAMC and was shipped off to Mesopotamia.

Few returned: Lieutenant Woodhouse fell in Mesopotamia, Lamaison on the Somme, Rogers at Arras with a posthumous DSO, and Stacey at some unrecorded spot. Then the German spring offensive of 1918 caught Major James Grieve MC, and Lieutenant Colonel Harold Roffey DSO. But the Germans no longer had adequate resources to exploit the breakthrough, so that the Allies, with the support of fresh American reserves, inflicted defeat after defeat on the Kaiser's exhausted army until the armistice of 11th November 1918. Even then, Gervaise Peters, who had survived the Mesopotamia campaign against the Turks, was killed in action on India's North West frontier in January 1920. His name is included in the eighty-eight listed on Merstham's granite war memorial, a depressingly large number for such a small village, which compares for example, with thirty-three on Chipstead's. The memorial was restored in 1986, but without amending its idiosyncratic spelling and sequence. As in the case of many another village, the funds raised for the war memorial were sufficient to provide a village hall as well. It was seven years later before work started on building the village Club and Hall so that the foundation stones then commemorated a more recent tragic loss of Merstham's young. For John Richardson JP a hop merchant of Harps Oak on London Road North, lost first one nineteen-year-old daughter, Katharine, in 1924, and then the other, Diana, also at nineteen, coincidentally on the same day as seventeen-year-old Joy Weir, in 1929.

Lord Hylton had been a Lord-in-Waiting to George V in the wartime coalition ministry. His heir, William, joined the

Coldstream Guards before the end of the war. His civilian brother, Thomas, died tragically in 1918, before his eighteenth birthday. Three of Agatha's sons, cousins of the Jolliffes, had survived. The eldest, Captain Ronald Fellowes MC of the Rifle Brigade, had served throughout the war in Flanders. Possibly while recuperating from his having been wounded, he met and married a Mildred King in 1916, before returning to command his battalion, earn a DSO and be promoted to Major. She in the meantime, was housed by her new relatives in Merstham, at Barn Cottage on School Hill. In 1921 Agatha's husband was made Lord Ailwyn. Three years later, Major Fellowes succeeded to his father's new peerage and the family's Norfolk seat. Lady Ailwyn was widowed in 1936 and spent the last thirty years or so of her life at Barn Cottage. Having no children, the title passed to Ronald's younger brothers and became extinct in 1988.

Understandably, the post-war period was one of substantial adjustment for Merstham. Not since the Southcotes left the village was there such a rapid removal of the senior residents: Sir Walter Roffey (he had been knighted for his wartime work) moved to East Grinstead in 1919, and then Lingfield when he became President of the London Corn Trade Association. He, the last of the Roffeys of Merstham, died there in 1940. The Stephens moved from Rookwood to Coppice Lea, but not before giving five acres of their Albury estate for the Recreation Ground. Lottie Stephens was an exceptionally able-spirited woman, co-founder of the local Women's Institute and Nursing Association. Further down the road Ringwood became a boys' school, the Hawthorns, following the departure of the remaining Grieves. When William Grieve died in Putney in 1927 he was buried by St Katharine's, as was his daughter, Vera, in 1984. The Hicks, who had been the first to tour the front entertaining the troops during the war, also left Merstham, moving first to one, then another, London house. The Old Forge was, after all, where they spent their best and longest time, 'the dearest of them all'. Seymour was knighted in 1935, a somewhat late recognition of his talent (the following year Macintosh introduced its toffee and chocolate assortment, for 6d a quarter, under the same-based *Quality*

Street name). Paxton Watson died in about 1920, though his sister stayed on in Quality Street. The health of Reverend R. I. Woodhouse had steadily declined since the death of his only son and he retired to Reigate in 1921 where he died a year later. When St Katharine's churchyard was extended with the purchase of the plot between the railway and the A23 road, the lychgate was dedicated to the Woodhouse family. Co-incidentally South Merstham's vicar, William London, also died that year. His successor, Reverend Henry Baker, had not been long in residence before his wife died and was buried by St Katharine's. As with the most recent, so too the longest lasting resident, when the following year Mrs Pelly of Oakley, probably also the eldest resident, died. In a very short space of time, few of Merstham's pre-war characters remained.

There was less change in relation to Gatton's residents. Charles Jarvis, who got an OBE for his war effort, inherited his family's Lincolnshire seat following the death of his two senior cousins in 1919/21 and left Nutwood Lodge which was briefly occupied by a Major Gregson. Luckily for those who remained, Sir Jeremiah Colman continued his bounteous administration of Gatton. He had taken on the Presidency of Surrey County Cricket in 1916, but was happy to give it up to become Vice President in 1923, a post he enthusiastically enjoyed until his death nearly twenty years later. Among locals though, apart from his prowess at shooting (hitting his fourth pheasant before the first had hit the ground), it was his firework displays that were best remembered. Mr John Campbell had bought Upper Gatton from the Bensons by 1919. It was probably a relative of his that had married Sir Alfred Tritton, of the City bill broking family, and the Upper Gatton estate was soon occupied by the Trittons with their three children. In 1924 Colman's only son and heir married Edith Tritton from Upper Gatton and the couple are next found with their baby daughter in Gomshall, between Dorking and Guildford. It was a good year for weddings. Rosamund, the late Mr Woodhouse's youngest daughter, was well known locally, especially for organising the local Scouts, so that most of the village turned out to see her marriage to Captain Charles Morris, another 'Piffer' as those who served

The Colman family 1928

in the Indian Frontier Rifles were called, whom she had met during the war in Salonika.

One only has to see some of the old Pathe News films to be reminded that the 1920s were a period of frantic activity internationally as well as nationally. With Imperial Airways based at Croydon, a well-off resident of Merstham was suddenly within easy reach of the Continent, and indeed, by hopping from one airport to another, any part of the British Empire. This sudden shrinkage of travelling time caught the popular imagination as vividly as a future generation's realisation of space travel. Ideas move as rapidly as those with them. International Socialism spread from Russia across Europe only to receive a check in Britain with the failure of the General Strike of 1926. But by then the United States had already taken over as the world's dominant nation. In England the twin influences of American democracy and Socialist egality encouraged the hopes and aspirations of the new generation of employees. Gradually only the larger establishments kept any household staff, while the demand for better housing pushed the urban dweller further away from the City centre, leaving the high density Victorian terraces for the new semi-detached developments in the nearby countryside. Such 'ribbon' development naturally followed the main road and rail links. Merstham could not fail to be caught up in it. Between the Ordnance Surveys of 1920 and 1932, Merstham continued its pre-war growth with the development of London Road North, the rest of Church Hill, Brook and Albury Roads, the Western side of Nutfield Road, Devon, Deans and Bourne Roads. The main beneficiaries were the local building firms of S. J. Francis & Son, R. Whitaker Ltd and of course, Pink & Oram Ltd of Endsleigh Road. The Pink family moved around the village, including Highwood in Church Hill and the Gables in Quality Street, and are now at rest under a suitably pink marble tomb by St Katharine's. Merstham House was still occupied by Mrs Walker and some of her family, while one of her sons-in-law, William Nicholson of Tootals the shirtmakers, bought Church Hill House at this time. Dr Walter Weir moved to the Bell House on London Road South, while Merstham's latest rector, Reverend Arthur Robinson, also kept on the move, transferring to Johannesburg in 1926. He must have liked Merstham, though, as his ashes were buried here in 1945.

There can be no doubt that Merstham society was enriched by the newcomers to the parish of this period. The new rector, for example, was nothing less than a retired bishop. The Right Reverend Eyre Chatterton was sixty-six when he came to St Katharine's in 1926, having only just resigned his post as bishop of Nagpur in India. His career is illustrated by his publications: *History of the Church of England in India since the early days of the East India Company, Story of Gondwana, Fifty Years Mission Work in Chota Nagpur* and *Mesopotamia Revisited*, the last named being written while he was Deputy Chaplain General to the Mesopotamia Forces in 1917. Despite his age, he was an imposing character, well remembered by those who met him during his brief tenure here. He retired in 1931 to the Queen's Gate House in Richmond.

Most newcomers, though, were typically City folk who

MERSTHAM CRICKET CLUB 1937
(v. Reigate Priory)
Back row: W. Smith (Umpire), C.J. Wilson, F. Mace, G.H. Lunge, N. Thorne, C. Bull. *Middle row:* C.H. Pink, C.A. Pink, C. Bowring (Captain), H. Forman. *Bottom row:* R. F. Bugler, N.H. Bowring

could afford to leave the urban smog for the cleaner air of the Surrey Hills. By 1925 the new Southern Railway group had electrified the Brighton line as far as Stoats Nest and it was only a matter of time before the cleaner, more frequent, commuter service extended to Merstham and beyond. Despite the Surrey Hills area becoming known as the 'Stockbroker Belt', Arthur Moy of Tangledown on Rockshaw Road, was Merstham's sole representative of this profession. Further along the same road Cyril Bowring of C. T. Bowring & Co, the shipping and insurance group, moved into The Georgian House in 1925 with his family, soon becoming captain of the village cricket team, which at that time was the main focus of village society. Further along Rockshaw Road, Ash Pollard was built for Harold Webbe, the founder of a hire purchase company that became Mercantile Credit and who had recently become a member of the London County Council. At the far end of Rockshaw Road, near Rockshaw House, was Chaldon Rise. This house was occupied by Stephen Watney, whose family had been closely involved with the Mercers' livery company. His uncle, Colonel Sir Frank Watney, was its clerk (the chief administrator of the company's affairs) from 1919 to 1940, and both Stephen and his father took their turn as Master. His mother had brought Leigh Place into the family and it was in this connection that his father, Sir John Watney, included in its history details of a fellow Mercer, Copley of Gatton, for the Surrey Archaeological Society. Sir John had lived at Shermanbury House in Reigate until his death in 1923, but it was appropriate that his elder surviving son should end up in Merstham.

Rockshaw Road was not exclusively populated by City gentlemen. Picket Wood had been sold by Miss Watson to General Sir Walter Campbell, then Quarter Master General to the Forces. He came from the same breed of Scottish Ulstermen that produced Lawrence and Montgomery, but was unusual for his generation in having been to Cambridge University before joining the army. Having seen action with the Gordon Highlanders in the late Victorian campaigns on the North West Frontier, he got his first staff post at Paardeburg in the South African War. He served on the Western Front and was one of the architects of the successful withdrawal from the Gallipoli beach-head. His main achievement, though, was his staff work in supporting Allenby's rapid advance from Egypt to Turkey. By 1918 Campbell was responsible for the maintenance in the field of over a quarter of a million men and their animals. Adjusting to the peacetime bureaucracy of the War Office must have been difficult for him. A colleague described him as having a 'strong personality with some obstinacy in its composition'. On the other hand 'he never bore anyone any ill-will, and disliked intensely any form of publicity or self advertisement. His real happiness was always to be found with his family and friends'. He retired at sixty-nine in 1927 but stayed at Picket Wood with his wife until his death nine years later. Their tomb by St Katharine's is a modest affair, with little to distinguish it from that of any other

General Sir Walter Campbell
(Courtesy of the National Portrait Gallery)

Merstham resident.

Merstham's development would have been greater were it not for the then responsible attitude of the main landowner, Lord Hylton, who was also a fellow of the Surrey Archaeological Society. After the death of Mrs Walker in 1928, he advertised Merstham House for letting. 'This Surrey residence is noted for the beauty of its gardens'. But with the country so unsettled, few would make this sort of commitment. Baldwin's Conservative government was replaced by Ramsay MacDonald's ministry, followed within months by the American-led Great Crash of 1929. The year was memorable locally as Dr Weir was run over by a car outside Bell House, the injuries being sufficient for him to have to have his leg amputated five years later, and his only daughter Joy died the same day as Diana Richardson. In the midst of the subsequent depression, in 1931 Lord Hylton's only son, William, married Perdita, one of the late Raymond Asquith's daughters (who had become a Catholic only the year before). Although the couple were not based in Merstham, they did make use of it from time to time.

Despite the very welcome electrification of the railway, the village was losing a lot of its rural charm. With a population in 1931 of 4,500, it threatened to become a town and the Surrey Review Order of 1933 deprived the village of its independence dividing it between Banstead and Reigate boroughs (a decidedly mixed blessing as each part was then on the periphery of its local authority, and remains so even after the merger of Reigate and Banstead boroughs in 1974). Lottie Stephens was elected Merstham's first Councillor to Reigate. Public concern was mounting over the effect of the unfettered development of the period and the London County Council's Green Belt Scheme of 1933 was launched with a lot of home counties' support. One of the main proponents was Harold Webbe of Rockshaw Road who was chairman of the LCC in 1934. Nevertheless Lord Hylton was over seventy and mindful of the effect of the new Estate Duty on some of his peers. In September 1933 *The Times* carried a notice: 'Merstham Manor Estate, 2,700 acres along the Brighton Road, Lord Hylton's property, is to be developed residentially, and instructions have been given to Messrs R.H. & R.W.

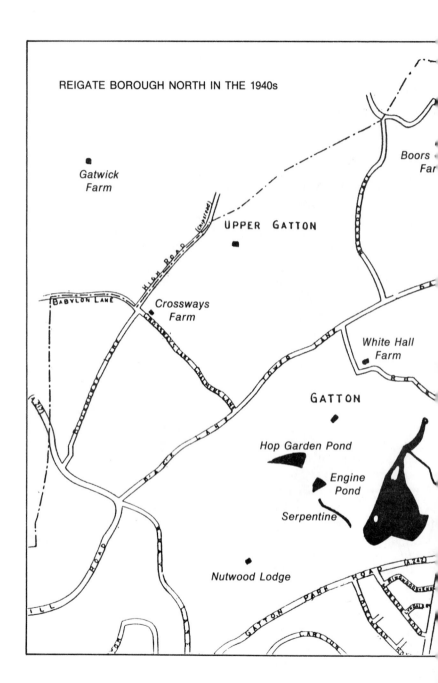

REIGATE BOROUGH NORTH IN THE 1940s

Gatwick
Farm

Boors
Far

UPPER GATTON

BABYLON LANE

Crossways
Farm

White Hall
Farm

GATTON

Hop Garden Pond

Engine
Pond

Serpentine

Nutwood Lodge

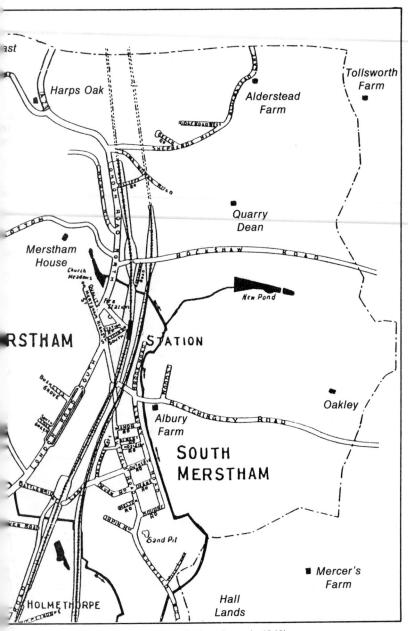

Map of Merstham (c.1940)

Clutton, Reigate, and Messrs J.D. Wood & Co.' (Mr Toms at Whitmore on Rockshaw Road was a partner of the latter London firm). Happily it was not to be and five years later the Green Belt Act became law, Harold Webbe getting a well-deserved knighthood. By then Shepherds Hill, London Road South and Orpin Road (after *Pin*k & *Or*am Ltd) had been developed, the main common feature being the by now standard provision for garaging a car. The few residences on Harps Oak Lane were also built at this time, Woodfield Place being occupied by a refugee from Merstham House, Hector Walker MC. Curiously, Merstham Lodge, across the lane from Woodfield Place, was built as a royal retreat for Princess Arthur of Connaught. She was a Duff and this horror of strangers was, according to Duff Cooper, a family trait.

In contrast Gatton had suffered a gradual decline in population. The estate however was maintained as well as ever until in February 1934, while Sir Jeremiah was abroad on holiday, disaster struck. Gatton Hall caught fire and, although his staff managed to save some of the portable valuables, the building was gutted. The fire had started in a cellar and, fuelled by the oak and cedar panelling, swept through the entire building destroying the valuable contents of the library and Monson's fine marbled hall. The portico remained and was incorporated in the rebuilding of 1936. Although keeping to a classical style, the new building, designed by Sir Edwin Cooper, is much more functional, reflecting the wish of seventy-six-year-old Sir Jeremiah that it be of some alternate use after his death. When Reverend Rogers retired in 1937, after forty-three years as rector, it was agreed that Gatton parish become the responsibility of Merstham's fifty-five-year-old rector, Reverend A. E. Wilkinson MC. He had earned his MC while senior chaplain of the 47th London division in Flanders. After the war he had a Croydon parish before coming to Merstham, as did Reverend Grosvenor, the present incumbant. Rogers stayed on in Rockshaw Road with his family.

Although the Jolliffes rarely visited Merstham, it was not until 1935, when they removed the iron gates at the Quality Street entrance of Merstham House to Ammerdown, that they were thought of as absentee landlords. This seems to have etched itself on the village consciousness much more than the more newsworthy items of the time such as the destruction of Crystal Palace or the abdication of Edward VIII. Other changes in the parish were more gradual. The East Surrey Water Company is generally considered responsible for the lowering of the water table so that the village stream that used to flow from below St Katharine's, with a tributary from Picket's Wood, beside Brook Street and south through Albury manor, was reduced to a trickle. The water mill behind the telephone exchange was redundant and in 1938 was demolished (the mill pond lasted until the motorway was built through it thirty-seven years later). At the time Jolliffe Cottages, the row of stone-terraced houses behind the Jolliffe Arms, were rated as no longer suitable for habitation. The occupants were rehoused in Wood Street and their former homes demolished. Presumably some of them still worked at the Greystone lime works, which was linked to Merstham station by a spur line. The little steam engine for it was housed by Quarry Dean and called 'Gervaise' after Mrs Peter's son.

As events in Continental Europe threatened to precipitate the next World War, Chamberlain tried to buy time for Britain to repair the damage done to its armed forces by twenty years of semi-pacifist government. Among other things he brought back Sir John Anderson from Bengal (a hotbed of terrorism) to be his Home Secretary and Minister of Home Security in time for the outbreak of hostilities. Sir John was a widower and bought Picket Wood in Rockshaw Road from Lady Campbell more as a base for his two children than as a home for himself. As can be imagined he was extremely busy for the few months he held this office. Yet he is best remembered for one of his less important accomplishments. For it was he that commissioned the cheap and simple air raid shelter that bore his name. In May 1940 Winston Churchill replaced Chamberlain as head of the National Government, but had sufficient regard for Sir John Anderson to make him Lord President of the Council, arbiter of the nation's most secret deliberations. The following year Sir John married Ava Wigram and lived at their Westminster house within easy reach of the War

Office. He became Chancellor of the Exchequer in 1943 and after his retirement to Sussex was made Lord Waverley in 1952. Merstham's representation in Parliament was otherwise maintained by Sir Harold Webbe who had been Conservative MP for Westminster since 1939.

With conscription, the new generation in Merstham did not have the choice available to their fathers at the start of the previous war. Although no longer connected with the area, it is appropriate to note that Percy Grieve joined the Middlesex regiment, the same as that of his father. In place of their own young men, Merstham received units of the Canadian Army in June 1940. The remains of the British Expeditionary Force had just been evacuated from Dunkirk (including young Christopher Weir of the Cameronians who was later awarded an MC for his gallant behaviour there) and the 1st Canadian division under the command of General McNaughton was the only major force available for the defence of Britain. Merstham House, Rockshaw, Wychwood and Nutwood Lodge were taken over by the Canadians and a camp of Nissan huts was established in the woods either side of Harps Oak Lane, between Boors Green and Cold Roast farms. With the arrival of a second Canadian division in Sussex, General McNaughton was promoted to command the seventh Corps, while Brigadier Pearkes VC, DSO, MC took over the First Division. In addition to the regular and territorial forces, the government established a Home Guard composed of those otherwise too old or too young for the services. The result was a curious mixture of attitudes and skills, well portrayed in the later television comedy series 'Dads' Army'. The local Home Guard had its headquarters at Reigate, the Merstham contingent being commanded by Cyril Bowring, with Sydney Figg of Mill House as his second in command. Their chief concern was the security of the railway which acted as the main conduit for men and materials to the coast. Extra sidings were constructed at Merstham between the two main lines.

In the battle of Britain that September, Merstham had its first direct involvement in warfare in 300 years, with a fine view of the daily aerial combats, many involving the Hurricans of 253 Squadron from the nearby Kenley airfield. One of their fighters crashed at Merstham and the wounded pilot, F.O. Gowers was taken to a Caterham hospital. Bombs landed all over the North Downs, the main local casualty being Cold Roast farm. The railway was the target. A land mine dropped by parachute in April 1941 destroyed All Saints church and vicarage, killing ten people, most of whom had been standing at the nearby bus stop. In due course the Royal Canadian Engineers salvaged enough of All Saints' timbers to build a replacement church (now Canada Hall) for a grateful village. Sadly Reverend George Wolfendale, their chaplain responsible for getting the hall built, was later killed in action in France. Most deaths locally, though, were still through natural causes. Sir Alfred Tritton of Upper Gatton had died the day before Britain declared war and within a couple of years Sir Jeremiah Colman at eighty-two underwent a serious operation. He never fully recovered and died in January 1942, much missed. Despite his gift to the National Trust, Estate Duty claimed £984,000 of his £1,671,000 estate.

Colonel Charles Morris, who had bought Merlebank on Church Hill for his family to be near their grandmother in The Cottage, Quality Street, was with his Piffers in North Africa. In June 1942, in the retreat to El Alamein, he was captured and brought before Field Marshal Rommel: 'Morris asked leave of Rommel to bid good-bye to his men. This was granted and speaking to them in Urdu, he gave them instructions about escaping. As the prisoners were being marched off under an Italian escort, a British armoured car suddenly appeared its machine guns firing. The Italian guards took cover and the prisoners scattered.' Then, as Colonel Morris said, 'we seized a few British lorries which the Germans had captured, while the guards were asleep, and drove off. During the day we overtook on the road two German brigades. When challenged, we shouted, blew the lorries' horns and waved our arms forward. We were allowed to pass, and the German military traffic being well trained, moved into the side of the road to allow what appeared to be an important convoy to pass'.[18] They were picked up by a New Zealand patrol and presently Morris was interviewing Auchinleck. A truly international incident. The battle of El Alamein marked the turning point of the war. The German army was soon in retreat in North Africa and later in Russia. On 19th August the Canadians made an expensive raid on Dieppe, losing most of their second Division. As a demonstration to the Russians that it was too early to start a second front, it was a success, but that would have been small consolation to the Canadians around Merstham. Nor did it relieve the strain of perpetually waiting for action. Then, in 1943 the First Division joined the Eighth Army in its invasion of Sicily and General McNaughton, who had argued with his Canadian Minister about splitting up his divisions, was replaced by General Crerar.

The Canadians apart, the most senior serving officer locally was the Naval Paymaster General, Rear Admiral Sir David Lambert of The Red House in Rockshaw Road. He was head of naval accounts until 1942 when he joined the Directorate of Economy in the Ministry of Supply. Appropriately enough, he had served throughout the previous war with the Royal Canadian Navy, and then married a Canadian girl from Victoria. Next door, the Bowring family had strong Newfoundland connections, and the elder son Derrick had been with the family business there before war called him back. Although the Lambert on the war memorial is not a relative (Sir David Lambert was childless), the Bowring is: Norman, the younger son, was reported 'missing from air operations' after a bombing raid over Leipzig in December 1943. Captain Vine of Valencia lost his elder son. It was 1944 before an invasion of occupied France was fully prepared. By then the Canadian Army had spread into camps at Pendell (wooden huts built for conscript training in 1939) and Alderstead Heath, while Gatton had been taken over as a training centre. General Montgomery was in charge of Twenty-first Army Group (First Canadian and Second British Armies) with its headquarters at Reigate Hill, and of the Normandy landings. The Canadians successfully established their Juno beach-head, leaving Merstham almost empty. At least two Merstham girls (Miss Toms and Miss Merritt) had married Canadians during their stay, and the village would have shared their concern for the safety of their transatlantic visitors.

That June the first German VI flying bombs, or 'doodlebugs', landed on London. In order to minimise the capital's casualties barrage balloons were flown from the top of the Downs and false information was given as to the VIs' accuracy so that later flights were launched at the North Downs rather than the more crowded City suburbs. One demolished Innisfree on Rockshaw Road, killing all inside, that August. Mrs Spalding's daughter, a graduate chartered accountant, was luckily away at the time. Another destroyed a cottage next to the Council depot on Nutfield Road. There was some damage on Church Hill, Shepherds Hill and Bletchingley Road, but only slight. Within a year the war in Europe was over. In August 1945 thirty-three names were added to the village war memorial, a lot more rapidly than after the previous war and, judging from the service graves in the churchyard, not as comprehensive. The ratio of roughly three to one, First to Second World War casualties, is typical of memorials all over rural England.

Only gradually did village life return to normal. The problems of power and food shortages were exacerbated in early 1947 when the area experienced the severest weather recorded this century. With constant blizzards and extreme frost the village was under snow from 24th January to 10th March. When the thaw eventually came it caused a landslide in the railway cutting. That apart, there remained a great deal to do to reconstruct the national economy, let alone that of the Continent. It is not really surprising that the tidying up operation took so long, and indeed there are still 'pill boxes' in the grounds of Upper Gatton. Gatton Hall looked like a deserted Officers' Mess, which is how Pevsner's Guide describes its design, and it was sold in 1948 to the Royal Alexandra & Albert School, a long established charitable foundation for the education of children of members of the armed services. It built enough boarding houses to handle over 500 pupils, of which no more than two thirds now have a services' parent. Both Merstham House and Upper Gatton House were up for sale but such large houses were not attractive in the post-war climate. In particular four years of bombing had made property in and about London considerably less attractive than their

Merstham House from the air

provincial alternative (those who bought despite this attitude did extremely well in later years). Also five years of Army occupation left its mark. Both properties were eventually demolished, the stable block of Upper Gatton being converted into a more saleable house. Nutwood Lodge was also pulled down, the woodland being given to the National Trust, while Rockshaw House was left in such poor condition it had to be rebuilt. It was years after the war was over before the economy recovered from the wartime austerity. Rationing, for example, continued for bread until August 1948, clothes until March 1949, soap until September 1950 and sugar until September 1953. It was the determination of this generation that their children should not have to put up with the same hardship, that ensured the next generation would 'never have it so good'.

12

NOT-SO-GREEN BELT
1949-1979

The post war years have been characterised by an
unprecedented degree of government authority. The willing-
ness to accept this stems from the initial benefits that could
be attributed to the more sophisticated system of ministerial
control. It was no accident that the Second World War had
a considerably lower cost to Britain in terms of human lives
that did the First, nor that the national economy suffered
less trauma compared to the situation thirty years previously.
The authoritarian manner in which Churchill led the
country to victory may not have endeared him to the
electorate (so that the Labour Party won the 1945 election
with an overall majority for the first time). But most voters
were supportive of Attlee's brief government rapidly
introducing the National Health Service, as well as bringing
the Railways, Airlines, Coal, Gas, Electricity and Steel
industries into government ownership. It has taken another
thirty years for it to be accepted that the problems
associated with this 'public' ownership can outweigh the
benefits, but at the time it was a logical sequence to the
efficiency of the wartime economic structure.

Nor, as far as Merstham was concerned, was there the
sudden change of local families that occurred following the
previous war. Certainly the elder generation, such as
Reverend Rogers, Peter Stephens, Stephen Watney, Lord
Hylton and the Walker brothers, reached the end of their

allotted time (the last rector of Gatton was buried in his own parish and eighty-five year-old Watney rejoined his family in their Leigh plot). But the next generation remained in the locality: Walter Weir was still at the Bell House, while Anthony Stephens, who a decade earlier had married Rosemary, Sir Harold Webbe's daughter, took over Coppice Lea from his late father. Michael Callow, who had spent part of his childhood at Nutfield, had married Sophia Watson the daughter of Lord Thankerton, before the war and brought her to Merstham from where he continued to commute to work in the City. From 'Dianns' in Beech Road, off Shepherds Hill, they moved via Chaldon to Relf House on Rockshaw Road. By 1960 Callow was working nearer home with British Gelco Engineering at Edenbridge. After his death in 1977 his widow moved to Quality Street. His son John now lives at Mercers Farm appropriately between Merstham and Nutfield. Similarly Sonia Bowring who had been brought up at The Georgian House, married Ronald Prentice and moved along Rockshaw Road to Standish. They had both had an interesting war, he having spent the latter part of it in Special Operations with the Yugoslav partisans. In no time he inherited his father-in-law's responsibilities as captain of the village cricket club. Colonel Morris DSO had also had an interesting war, only to see the regiment in which he had spent thirty years, transferred to the newly-independent pakistan. He was only fifty-two at his death in 1950.

There was also a welcome influx of young couples new to the area, many of whom, in keeping with what was fast becoming a tradition in Merstham, were of Scottish origin. John Alexander was one of four sons of Sir William Alexander, Conservative MP for Glasgow and Managing Director of the family business, Charles Tennant & Co., the chemical company whose chimney stack, 'Tennants Stalk', used to dominate Victorian Glasgow. The holding company, Tennants Consolidated Ltd, is based in London so that when John left the army after the war, he joined the other commuters of Rockshaw Road. He bought first West Cross from Sydney Figg in 1949, and moved twelve years later with his growing family to Oakwood. Sadly he was to die relatively young. His widow then moved into the Old Forge in Quality Street. The Merstham widows' traditional move to Quality Street had been established by the previous generation — Mrs Woodhouse in the 1920s and Lady Lambert and Mrs Nicholson more recently. Clavadel was bought from the Nicholsons by a stockbroker, Jock Hunter, who had ended up at the end of the war as a Colonel in the Gunners. Following demobilisation he resumed his position as a director of Messel & Co. and also became deputy chairman of Ranco Ltd. Appropriately enough, he soon swapped Clavadel for Tanglewood, the other stockbroker's house which suited Arthur Moy's widow when her son moved to Reigate. Another arrival in Rockshaw Road was Pierre Lachelin of The Mere. He was a director of Philip Hill, Higginson, Erlangers Ltd., one of the new merchant banks in the City, and which later merged to form Hill Samuel. The Lachelins were very much part of the village, contributing to St Katharine's and the Women's Institute. Their daughter Patsy later married Christopher Watney, grandson of the late Stephen Watney of Chaldon Rise. John Lee of Eagle Star Insurance was another City type who established his family in Merstham at this time. He started in Harps Oak Lane, at Field End, before later moving to Alderstead Farm. Not all the gentlemen settling in Merstham were businessmen. At thirty-nine Joseph Poole was one of Merstham's younger rectors when he joined the parish from Canterbury with his family following Mr Wilkinson's death in 1949. It was during his tenure that the separate parish of Gatton was formally merged in 1956 with that of Merstham. He is better remembered for his enthusiasm for good music, happily shared by those of the same generation. He was appointed Precentor of Coventry Cathedral in 1958. His successor, Mr Biddell, established a different sort of reputation on the cricket pitch.

The purpose of the Green Belt policy had been to contain the growth of London. This policy was reinterpreted after the war in terms of decentralising both people and jobs from crowded inner London. Paradoxically it was because it involved the relocation of people for whom there was otherwise insufficient council housing in London, that the London County Council was permitted to develop rural sites beyond the LCC area in what otherwise would have been an infringement of the Green Belt. The London County Council purchased several sites for this purpose, one such being the Stephens' Oakley farmland between South Merstham's Albury Road and Coppice Lea (Oakley itself became a Youth Centre). Sir Harold Webbe had retired from the LCC in 1945 but stayed on at his Rockshaw Road home overlooking the development of his successors. The estate was built between 1948 and 1950 and was described as 'the worst designed estate of the former LCC'[19] though it has since mellowed somewhat and does compare favourably with some of the later, higher density, council developments. In all 1,560 homes were built with attendant shops and schools, a pub called the Iron Horse after Merstham's earliest railway, a church dedicated to the Epiphany, and a chapel for Merstham's Baptist community to replace their tiny one on the High Street. Despite memories of the South Croydon rail crash of 1947, when thirty-one commuters were killed in a collision, there was no shortage of Londoners prepared to move out of the metropolis. There are still many who remember the great smog of 1952 when the urban mixture of smoke and fog reduced visibility to a point when all forms of London transport ceased to function. Pollution has since become less obvious and more widespread, but at the time Merstham represented a clearly healthier environment. With the estate complete Merstham's population had doubled to 9,000, a not insignificant part of Reigate borough. However from this time until the 1980s, when a large number of tenants bought their houses and the remaining properties were transferred to the borough on the abolition of the Greater London Council, Reigate borough council's interest in Merstham as a whole was understandably coloured by the presence of a rival local authority there. Yet the situation was far from unusual: The 1965 local government reform which brought the GLC into being, resulted in Surrey County's Kingston headquarters being within the GLC area. Subsequent reforms have done little to bring the local government structure more in line with the community's working and recreational patterns.

The other part of the government's policy was to decentralise jobs. To deal with this, eight new towns were planned in a 25-30 mile radius of central London. The only

Lord Benson

one south of London was Crawley. It was one of the members of the Crawley Development Board, Henry Benson, who decided that Merstham gave him the best base for his growing responsibilities and so acquired the Red House on Rockshaw Road from the Lamberts. Like his predecessor, he had served with the Ministry of Supply during the war, but as a recently qualified accountant dealing with the Royal Ordnance Factories. His reputation with senior members of the Labour party was to prove valuable individually and for his firm. After the war he soon became the main architect of the rapid growth of Cooper Brothers, challenging the then pre-eminent position of Deloittes, Price Waterhouse and Peat Marwick Mitchell as the top accountancy firms. He was appointed to the Fleck Committee examining the role of the National Coal Board, and thus was a natural choice as member of the later Wilson committee on extractive industries. He became senior partner of Cooper Brothers, was knighted, and elected President of the English Institute of Chartered Accountants while still at the Red House, but moved to Sussex with the coming of the motorways. He is now a life peer and has written a brief autobiography, with sadly no mention of the village in which he brought up his family.

Despite Suez and the 'Cold War', the next generation were growing up in a more secure Britain, guaranteed by 'the bomb' and educated, as much by the media as at school, in a strongly moral manner. Interest rates were considered excessive if they reached seven per cent, and credit grew accordingly. Television hire spread rapidly and Merstham's initial difficulty in receiving the short wave signals from Crystal Palace was improved with a relay mast, additional to the radio mast, on Reigate Hill. It was a comfortable period of consolidation with few dramatic changes to the locality. In 1956 Major Christopher Weir MC married Elizabeth Duval (while a clergyman, Philip Duval, became chaplain of the Weir hospital in south London). Dr Weir had moved from the Bell House to the Barn House in Quality Street, followed shortly afterwards by his neighbour, Anthony Stephens, who donated a field to Merstham's Primary School in 1957 before moving back

Anthony Stephens

(again temporarily) to Coppice Lea. The School's head-master, Charles Agate, is otherwise worthy of note as having achieved a then record number of parachute jumps. Generally though, Merstham gentlemen were of a more sober disposition: John Leonard was a judge of the South Eastern circuit when he bought Field End from the Lees. He has since been promoted, with a knighthood, to be a High Court Judge, Queens Bench Division, a worthy successor to Justice Southcote. Opposite him, Woodfield Place was occupied in the 1960s by Reverend Brian Kirk-Duncan while he was Principal of Becket College, and rector of one of the Wren City Churches, St Mary-at-Hill. Jeremiah Milles would have approved. Further West, Upper Gatton was acquired by another City gentleman, Christopher Price of the Credit Insurance Association Ltd., to the evident benefit of the estate. He was forty when he became its Managing Director in 1979 and not much older when he took it into the Hogg Robinson Group. At this time, Basil West, who was to become Director General of the Automobile Association before the end of the period under review, acquired Clavadel on Rockshaw Road. These were just a few of the gentlemen of many different professions who made their home in Merstham and Gatton prior to the nationwide lurch into a regency style liberality which questioned their moral values, and the equally sudden increase in inflation which eroded the real value of their capital.

There were also more tangible changes affecting the locality. Inevitably the government had to address the problems posed by the growing road and air travel. Gatwick airport expanded rapidly in the 1950s taking pressure off London's main Heathrow airport and permit-ting the closure of Croydon and Blackbushe airports. The newly-formed British Railways built a new station beside the airport while the more difficult task of providing a motorway link, the M23, reached the planning stage. The Conservative governments of the fifties gave motor-way construction a low priority, so it was not until the return of a Labour government in 1964 that the plans were brought before the public. In 1967 it was announced that the first stage of London's orbital road, the M25, was

Gatton coomb 1954

planned to link up with the M23 at Merstham. It is hard to imagine now, but the Holmesdale Valley between the North Downs and the Greensands ridge used to be considered 'in the opinion of many, the finest part of Surrey'. Contemporary guides used to recommend the 'quiet valleys east of Merstham' and the 'lovely chalk coombe' of Gatton Bottom to the west. They were within the designated Surrey Hills Area of Oustanding Natural Beauty, through which passed the government approved North Downs Way. But the main London to Brighton road was already extremely noisy and crowded, and crossing the High Street was 'a hazardous affair'. Given that the motorways were inevitable, the issue was how to obtain the minimum disruption to the environment. The projected route would require the destruction of Quarry Dean Farm and the houses at the end of Rockshaw Road, quite apart from imposing the sort of noisy barriers across the parish that would make the railway tame in comparison.

A Merstham Protection Society was formed led by such natural leaders as Ronald Prentice and John Lee, under the chairmanship of Brian Webbe of The Old Forge. They raised £2,000 to finance professional representation. While an alternative route was not accepted, the Ministry of Transport was prepared to take the motorway under, rather than over, the railway and A23. Not since the Jolliffe family had been resident, had there been such a cohesive representation of Merstham's interests. Apart from the relatively recently arrived members of this small community, there was the next generation of the more established families. Binks Nicholson, grandson of Andrew Walker, had inherited his mother's house, Meadowside in Quality Street. He was another chartered accountant, with Grand Metropolitan. Next door Courtney and Mary Morris had inherited their grandmother's house, and Mary Morris's history of Merstham, published at this time, helped promote the heritage of the village. John Biddell had been replaced by Philip Duval at the Rectory in 1966 and it was Philip Duval, whose own preferred form of transport was a motor scooter, who ensured the pedestrian bridge linking St Katharine's to Quality Street was not stepped, as originally proposed. Other pleas went unheeded, and, for example, the

187

surveyors soon learnt that the dangers of subsidence in Merstham's historic marshes were real enough.

For the lowering of the water table had hidden rather than eradicated the west moors to the east and south of the parish. A local builder such as Pink & Oram knew which fields were not worth developing. Wates is a more nationwide concern, and one might charitably assume it was ignorance that led this company to build a small estate South of Bourne Road at the height of the 1960s building boom. The degree of subsequent subsidence around Wycliffe Gardens meant Wates had to spend a fortune in underpinning, compensation and buy-backs. Generally, though, property has been the most lucrative investment since the war, and it is not surprising that there have been constant attempts by interested parties, including the Church Commissioners, to develop any spare patch of land locally. The Green Belt policy has been a very fragile protection. Colman's remaining interest in Gatton's fields were sold to local farming families just before the motorway cut through the middle of them. They remain efficiently farmed by Messrs Colebrook, Kent and Maiklem. The present Lord Hylton, who succeeded to the title in 1967, has gradually reduced his financial interest in the area, his Merstham estate company selling its assets bit by bit (including the fire-station and the Feathers), but generally with restrictive covenants to protect the quality of the parish. The more recent developments have tended to add rather than detract from the character of Gatton and Merstham (Battlebridge being the most glaring exception), with a fishing pond to the west of the cricket pitch and Mercers Park to the south of the Wates estate. The latter is a recreational lake and nature reserve made from one of the disused pits of British Industrial Sand Ltd, whose active works otherwise vie with Laporte's extractive works for domination of Nutfield Marsh.

Further north and east the motorway contractors proceeded with a technological efficiency that would have impressed the ghosts of the railway navvis of old. The efforts of the Merstham Society did have some benefit: In the wake of appropriate legislation, Surrey County Council designated the centre of Merstham a conservation area in December

1973. A year later the traffic through the village centre was reduced dramatically with the opening of the M23. The opening of the local section of the M25 to Reigate Hill in February 1976 had less impact than the completion of the whole motorway in October 1985. Since then there are few areas in the parish where one can escape the constant drone in the background. But with the highest mileage of motorway of any county in the country, and bracketed by London's two main airports, the whole of Surrey is afflicted with the same problem of 'noise pollution'. The cost of coping with this level of infrastructure is not helped by Gatwick and its revenue having been re-allocated to Sussex in the 1974 realignment of county boundaries.

There can be no doubt that there will be further changes in the locality, especially once the Channel Tunnel brings the Continent much closer, and that it will be only through some effort that the residents will be able to maintain the quality of life that they have come to expect. Having looked at the decision makers of Merstham and Gatton of the last 500 years, it is clear this is not a new situation; only the players have changed. Accordingly there can be no neat end to a tale such as this. Certainly one cannot stay long in Merstham or Gatton without realising the sense of stability and responsibility of this community. It is the influence of successive generations that have contributed to this, whether long established or of recent arrival, whether in the old hamlets or the newer estates. Some of the more obvious characters have been identified above; inevitably there will have been those who, either through modesty or by accident, have been missed. More important are those here now who will be making their contribution to the community in the future. When they do, it may be due in part to the local influence of those earlier generations whose actions have been worthy of record.

NOTES

1. Extract from Caterbury Wills, Folio 53, quoted in *Misc. Generalia et Heraldica*, 3rd Series, vol 1, 1904.
2. Donald Sharples' accounts for Thomas Copley of 1569 were kept for some time at St Olave's Church, Southwark. They were reproduced in *Collectanea Topographia et Genealogica vol VIII* printed by John Bowyer Nichols & Son in 1843.
3. The letter is in Kempe's *Losely MSS* p243 and is quoted in full in John Watney's *Account of Leigh Place, Surrey, and its Owners*, Surrey Arch. Soc. 1905.
4. Copley's letters were kept in the State Papers, Domestic, now a matter of public record. They were also separately published by a distant descendant, Richard Copley Christie, *Letters of Sir Thomas Copley* Roxburghe Club.
5. *Merstham Parish Registers*, as published by Rev. R. I. Woodhouse in 1902.
6. Reproduced in *Collectanea Topographia et Genealogica vol III* printed by John Bowyer Nichols & Son in 1843.
7. H. E. Malden, *The Victoria history of Surrey* 1905.
8. John Southcote's *Notebook, 1628-1637* was published by The Catholic Record Society.
9. *Calendar of State Papers Domestic, vol DXVI, Charles I*.
10. The Southcote Memoires were published in Morris's *Troubles of our Catholic Forefathers* 1872. These are quoted in Georgina Dawson's article *The Jacobite Southcotes of Witham* in the Essex Review 1954.
11. Rev. O. Manning & W. Bray, *The History & Antiquities of Surrey* 1905.
12. Historical Review *English Landownership 1680-1740*, 1940, quoted in G. M. Trevelyan's *English Social History* 1942.
13. Eric Parker, *East and Central Surrey, Highways & Byways* 1937.
14. Sir Frederick Eden, 1797, quoted in G. M. Trevelyan's *English Social History* 1942.
15. Extracts from the diaries are reproduced in Mary Morris' *History of Merstham* 1971.
16. Quoted in Doubleday & de Walden's *The Complete Peerage* 1929.
17. J. Vincent, *The Political Journals of Lord Stanley 1849-1869* 1978.
18. Compton Mackenzie, *Eastern Epic* 1951.
19. *The Shell Guide to Surrey*.

BIBLIOGRAPHY

Rental of the manor of Merstham in the year 1522, Lord Hylton, Surrey Archaeological Society 1907

Merstham Registers 1538-1812, Ed. Rev. R. I. Woodhouse 1902

Collectanea Topographica et Genealogica, J. Bowyer Nichols, 1836-43

The Visitations of Surrey 1530, 1572 & 1623, The Harleian Society, Ed. W. B. Bannerman, 1899

The Visitations of Surrey 1662-8, H. S., Ed. Sir G. W. Armytage, 1910

The Visitations of Sussex 1530, 1633/4, H. S., Ed. W. B. Bannerman, 1905

The Visitations of Lincolnshire vol 2 H. S., Rev. A. R. Maddison, 1903

Prerogative Court of Canterbury Wills 1547-1673, Harleian Soc., 1901-36

Some account of Leigh Place and its owners, J. Watney, Surrey Ar. Soc.

Register of Admissions, Middle Temple, Inner Temple etc

The Ordinance Book of the Merchants of the Staple, E. E. Rich, 1937

Misc Generalia et Heraldica, J. J. Howard, series, 1874-1904

Misc Generalia et Heraldica, W. B. Bannerman, series, 1904-1914

Calender of State Papers, Domestic 1547-1660

Natural History & Antiquities of the County of Surrey, J. Aubrey, 1719

The History & Antiquities of Surrey, Rev. O. Manning & W. Bray, 1808

History of Surrey, Thomas Allen, 1831

History of Surrey vol 4, Brayley & Britton, 1850

The Victoria History of Surrey, Ed. H. E. Malden, 1905

The Victoria History of Sussex, Ed. W. Page, 1907

Dictionary of National Biography, Ed. S. Lee, c.1888-92

Dictionary of American Biography, Ed. Johnson & Malone, 1930

East & Central Surrey Highways & Byways, Eric Parker, 1937

Surrey, London's Southern Neighbour, Ed. Arthur Mee, 1938

The Elizabethan House of Commons, J. E. Neale, 1949

History of Parliament: The Commons 1509-1558, S. T. Bindoff, 1982
    1558-1603, P. W. Hasler, 1981
    1660-1690, B. D. Henning, 1983
    1715-1754, R. Sedgewick, 1970
    1790-1820, R. G. Thorne, 1986

The Other Face, Philip Caraman, 1960

The Jacobite Southcotes of Witham, G. Dawson, The Essex Review, 1954

The Knights of England, W. A. Shaw, 1906

The Aldermen of the City of London, Rev. A. Beaven, 1913
The Rulers of London 1660-1689, London & Middlesex Arch'l. Soc., 1965
The Worshipful Company of Grocers, J. A. Rees, 1923
The Complete Peerage, G.E.C., Ed. Doubleday & de Walden, 1929
Reigate: Its story through the ages, W. Hooper, 1945
The Free Men of Charlewood, Sewill & Lane, 1951
Rascally spot of earth, a brief history of Gatton, F. Know, unpublished
The History of Merstham, H. M. Morris, 1971
A History of Chipstead, C. E. Pringle, 1984
Clive of India, M. Bence-Jones, 1974
Official Guide to the South Eastern Railway, G. Measom, 1858
Historical Geography of Railways of the British Isles, E. Carter, 1959
Retracing the First Public Railway, D. A. Bayliss, 1981
Down the Line to Brighton, M. V. Searle, 1988
The Railway Murders, J. Goodman, 1984
The Gentleman's Magazine for 19th Century, *Who's Who* for 20th Century
The Clergy List 1841, *Clergy Directory* 1881, & *Crockford* from 1894
The Peterloo Massacre, Joyce Marlow, 1969
Honour the Light Brigade, W. M. Lummis & K. G. Wynn, 1973
The Political Journals of Lord Stanley 1849-1869, Ed. J. Vincent, 1978
Just a Little Bit of String, Ellaline Terriss
The Red Book of Commerce, 1939
Eastern Epic, Compton Mackenzie, 1951
Who's Who in the City, 1964

INDEX

Pink 163,170,187
Pitches family 108,114
Poole, Rev. Joseph 180
Pope, Alexander 75,80
Portland, Duke of 94
        Earl of *see* Weston
Poynet, Bishop 23,25
Prentice 179,187
Price, Christopher 185
Prideaux, Thomas 46
Priors Mead 68,95

Quality Street 87,95,142,150,152,
   161,163,170,173,180,187

Ravis, Rev. Thomas 46
Redhill 61,126,129,142,146,156
Red House 174,183
Reeve, Joseph 68,71
Reigate Hill 84,135,154,155,174,183
Reigate Priory 20,60
Rennie, John 102,111,113-4,117,126,
   127
Richardson 159,167
Richbell, William 29
Rigge, Ambrose 67
Ringwood, Gatton Point 145,157,
   158,160
Robinson, Rev. A. 163
Rockshaw Road 148,152,156,158,
   164,167,170,179,187
Roffey family 115,123,140,149,154,
   156-60
Roffey, Horsham 13,21,59,64
Rogers family 152,158,170,178
Royal Alexander and Albert School
   175

St Albans, Duke of *see* Beauclerk
St Andrew's, G. 11,75,122,127
St Katharine's, M. 11,41,51,72,83,88,
   98,104,110,112,117,128,135,136,
   145,148,149,152,160-1,163,165,187
St Olave's, London 27,75
Sambourne, Rev. James 72,75,79
Sandys, Thomas 58
Saunders family 15,21,36
School Hill 87,129,160
Seaburne 52

Sellon, Percy 152
Sharples, Donald 29
Shaw Lefevre 120,128
Shelley family 14,15,17,21,29,35,42
Shelton, William 54
Shepherds Hill 103,111,124,142,147,
   154,170
Shove, Rev. Edmund 58
Simpson, Lady Ann 109,112
Skinner, James 25
Skinners' Livery Co. 144
Smith, Bishop R. 55
Smith, Fr. Nicholas 43
Somers, Lord *see* Cocks
Sonnibanke, Rev. Charles 51
Southcote family 41-43,50,52,55,57,
   59,60-3,67,68,70-83,185
South East Railway *see* LBSC etc
Southwell family 17,20,23-29,32,36,
   39,42,43,47
Stacey family 123,148,157-8
Stanihurst, Richard 47
Stephens family 151,154,160,167,
   178-9,181,183
Surrey Iron Railway 101-104,129

Tattershall family 83,88,91,94
Thompson family 70-72,74,76
Timperley, John 12,13,21
Topcliffe 47
Tritton family 161,173
Trower, Richard 144
Tyrwitt family 72,133
Tulse family 65,71
Turgis, Thomas 65-75,83

Upper Gatton 55,66,74,76,77,84,92,
   95,98,108,131,140,154,161,173,
   175-6,185

Waldegrave family 41,73
Walker family 131,149,156,158,167,
   170,178,187
Walpole family 81,131,136
Warwick, Countess of 117,122,128,
   129,131,144
Watney 165,178,180
Watson, Paxton 136,150-51,161
Webbe, Sir Harold 164,167-8,172,
   178,181